KV-589-661

Visual Science Encyclopedia

Earth and Space

▲ Columns of interstellar hydrogen gas and dust where new stars will eventually form. They are part of the Eagle Nebula, 7,000 light-years away from Earth.

How to use this book

Every word defined in this book can be found in alphabetical order on pages 3 to 47. There is also a full index on page 48. A number of other features will help you get the most out of the *Visual Science Encyclopedia*. They are shown below.

Here you will find the first word defined on any left-hand page.

Here you will find the last word defined on any right-hand page.

Each word is shown in bold so it is easy to find.

Each new letter of the alphabet is clearly marked to help you find the word you are looking for quicker.

Other words defined in the book are highlighted in bold.

Illustrations for some words complement the text and provide further information on a topic.

Plus, many entries point to related words of interest.

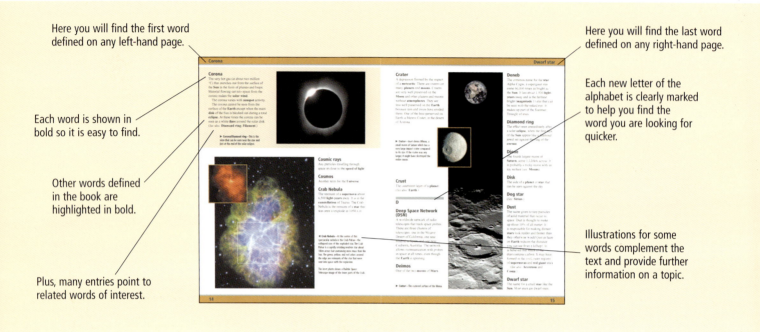

First published in 2002 by Atlantic Europe Publishing Company Ltd

Copyright © 2002 Atlantic Europe Publishing Company Ltd

All rights reserved. No part of this publication may be reproduced, stored in a retrieval system, or transmitted in any form or by any means – electronic, mechanical, photocopying, recording, or otherwise – without prior permission of the publisher.

Author
Brian Knapp, BSc, PhD

Art Director
Duncan McCrae, BSc

Senior Designer
Adele Humphries, BA, PGCE

Editors
Lisa Magloff, BA, and
Mary Sanders BSc

Illustrations
David Woodroffe and Julian Baker

Designed and produced by
EARTHSCAPE EDITIONS

Reproduced in Malaysia by
Global Colour

Printed in Hong Kong by
Wing King Tong Company Ltd.

Visual Science Encyclopedia
Volume 9 *Earth and space*
A CIP record for this book is available from the British Library

ISBN 1-86214-049-9

Picture credits
All photographs are from the Earthscape Editions photolibrary except the following:
(c=centre t=top b=bottom l=left r=right)

NASA cover, 3 (all except Mercury, Pluto and Uranus), 5tr, 5c, 6tr, 7r, 9, 11, 12tr, 14tr, 15c, 19t, 20, 21l, 22t, 22b, 23bl, 23br, 24tr, 24c, 24bl, 25r, 25b, 26, 27b, 28tr, 28c, 29b, 30bc, 30br, 32bc, 32br, 35, 36t, 37l, 37cr, 37br, 40bl, 42bl, 44cl, 46tc, 46tr, 47t, 47b; *Jeff Hester and Paul Scowen (Arizona State University) and NASA* 1, 14bl, 14cl; *USGS* 3 Mercury; *Dr R. Albrecht, ESA/ESO Space Telescope European Coordinating Facility/NASA* 3 Pluto, 34b; *Kenneth Seidelmann, US Naval Observatory/NASA* 3 Uranus; *Jason Ware* 4; *Susan Terebey (Extrasolar Research Corp.) and NASA* 10l; *NASA/John Trauger (Jet Propulsion Laboratory) and James Westphal (California Institute of Technology)* 10r; *Voyager 1, NASA* 15l; *NASA/JPL/University of Arizona* 20r; *Edward A. Guinness, Washington University in St. Louis* 28b; *H. A. Weaver, T. E. Smith (Space Telescope Science Institute) and NASA* 37t; *Kitt Peak National Observatory 0.9-meter telescope, National Optical Astronomy Observatories, courtesy M. Bolte (University of California, Santa Cruz* 41tr; *FORS Team, 8.2-meter VLT Antu, ESO* 44; *Philip James (University of Toledo), Steven Lee (University of Colorado) and NASA* 44tr; *STS 30 Crew and NASA* 46b.

This product is manufactured from sustainable managed forests. For every tree cut down, at least one more is planted.

A

Accretion

The accumulation of **dust** and gas to make large bodies. It is one of the most important processes in the formation of the **planets**. The early **Earth**, for example, is thought to have grown by this process, with **meteorites** and small **planetesimals** colliding with it regularly. The effect of the collisions was to heat the surface of the Earth and at the same time cover it with a blanket of dust that kept the heat in. In this way the Earth could have become hot enough to begin melting after growing to less than 15% of its final volume. All this may have occurred within a few hundred million years after the **Sun** was formed.

One or more planetesimals that struck the Earth are thought to have been about the same size as the early Earth. Some astronomers have suggested that the **Moon** could have been formed when a large chunk of the Earth was blasted away at the time of this collision. This might account for why the rocks on the Moon are similar to those found in the Earth's mantle.

Once accretion had caused the Earth's rocks to heat up to melting point, the metals in the rocks would have begun to sink towards the centre of the Earth to form the core. At the same time, this would have released enough gravitational energy to generate yet more heat. In this way the core became even hotter. Radioactive decay of elements brought to the planet during accretion could have added to the heating.

Mercury

Venus

Moon

Earth

Mars

Jupiter

Saturn

Uranus

Neptune

Pluto

Adrastra

The second closest, and one of the largest, of **Jupiter's** satellite rocks, some 25km across, and on the edge of the **Jovian** ring. It orbits 129,000km above the **planet's** surface and is probably important in keeping the rocks of the ring in place, acting as a '**shepherd moon**'.

Albedo

The amount of light reflected from an object. The higher the albedo, the more light it reflects, and the brighter it looks. Many features on the **planets** in the **Solar System** are seen in patterns of light and dark. By comparing the way the landscapes reflect light, scientists can estimate some properties of these remote surfaces.

Alpha Centauri

A bright triple **star** and the closest bright star system to the **Sun**, at about 4.3 **light-years** distance. The two brighter stars revolve around each other every 80 years, with the third revolving around them far more slowly. The brightest star is similar to the Sun. One of the other stars is more red than the Sun, and the third is a **red dwarf** star.

Alpha Centauri appears from Earth as the third **brightest star** (the brighter stars being **Sirius** and Canopus). It is visible to anyone in the night sky who is looking from south of 40°N latitude.

Alpha Crucis

The **brightest star** in the Crux **constellation**. It is actually a double **star**, some 510 **light-years** from the **Earth**.

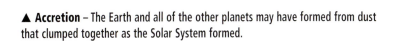

▲ **Accretion** – The Earth and all of the other planets may have formed from dust that clumped together as the Solar System formed.

Altair

The 12th **brightest star** in the sky, 16 **light-years** from the **Earth**. It is visible as part of a triangle of stars, of which the others are **Deneb** and **Vega**.

Andromeda

A **constellation** found in the northern sky and containing the **Andromeda Galaxy**.

Andromeda Galaxy

The nearest spiral **galaxy** to the **Solar System**, lying 2.3 million **light-years** away. It has a mass 400 billion times that of our **Sun**, which makes it just a little more massive than our galaxy. It stretches over an area of 150 light-years.

▼ **Andromeda Galaxy** – The nearest galaxy to the Solar System. Like the Solar System, it has more stars near the centre, giving it a bulging appearance.

Angstrom

A tiny unit of length 10^{-10} metres (that is, 10 divided by 10 trillion metres) and used to measure the wavelengths of light. The symbol for angstrom is Å. It is named after the 19th-century Swedish physicist Anders Jonas Ångström. It has been replaced by the nanometer, which is ten times larger.

Antipodal point

The point of a **planet** directly opposite any other point. For example, on **Earth** the North Pole is the antipodal point to the South Pole.

Aphelion
(*See:* **Apse**.)

Apoapsis
(*See:* **Apse**.)

Apogee
(*See:* **Apse**.)

Apollo group
A group of small **asteroids**, less than 5km across, that cross the **Earth's orbit**.

▶ **Apollo project** – Footprint on the Moon.

▶ **Apollo project** – Neil Armstrong, the first person to walk on the Moon.

Apollo project
The name of the **NASA** programme that landed people on the **Moon**. The space vehicle designed to **orbit** the Moon was called Apollo, and it was launched by a **Saturn V** rocket. Apollo was crewed by three **astronauts**. Once in orbit, the **lunar module**, containing two of the astronauts, detached itself from the Apollo spacecraft and powered its way to the surface of the Moon. The first person to walk on the Moon on July 20, 1969, was Neil Armstrong, whose quote, as he stepped onto the lunar surface, was 'One small step for man, one giant leap for mankind.'

The Apollo spacecraft was also used to take crews to the **Skylab** space station and to join with the Russian **Soyuz** spacecraft.

Apse, apsis
Most orbiting bodies in the **Universe** follow elliptical (oval) **orbits**. An apse is the point either nearest or farthest from the focus (centre) of the orbit. The line of apsides joins the two farthest points. It forms the major **axis**.

The point nearest the focus is the **periapsis**, and the point farthest from it is the apoapsis. In the case of the **Sun** the periapsis is called the **perihelion**, and the apsis is called the aphelion. For bodies in orbit around the **Earth** the words **perigee** and **apogee** are used. For bodies in orbit around **Jupiter** perijove and apojove are used, and for bodies orbiting a **star** other than the Sun periastron and apastron are used.

Ariel

The fourth largest **satellite** of **Uranus**, 1,158km across. It takes just over two days for Ariel to **orbit** Uranus at a distance of 191,000km from the surface. It is an icy world, but there are large trenches and **craters** on its surface, suggesting that it may have been geologically active in the past.

Aristotle

Aristotle lived in Greece between 384 and 322 BC. He was one of the most outstanding thinkers and scientists of all time.

He was fascinated by many things, including the nature of the **Earth** and the way in which **planets** and **stars** moved in the sky.

He was the first to figure out that the Earth was a sphere and not a flat disc, as had previously been believed. He also made the first calculation of the diameter of the Earth.

From his studies, and from the works of earlier writers, he concluded that the Earth was the centre of the **Universe** and that the other planets, the **Sun** and all of the other **stars** revolved around it.

This view was changed slightly by **Ptolemy**, but was unchallenged until the work of **Copernicus** and **Galileo** in the 17th century AD. By this time the Earth as the centre of the Universe was a traditional part of the thinking of the Christian church. Changing these theories to the ones we now believe in was a difficult process, as is reflected in the life of Galileo.

Asteroid number

Asteroids are each numbered as they are discovered. There is no other meaning to the number.

Ida shown in the photo at the top right is asteroid number 243.

Asteroids

There are many rocky fragments in our **Solar System** that have never been swept together to form **planets**. Most of the larger ones – called asteroids – swarm in a belt between **Mars** and **Jupiter**, although a few have paths that take them near the **Earth**; they are known as the **Apollo group**.

To understand how asteroids were formed, it is important to look back to the formation of the Solar System. Very early on in the history of the Solar System, when all of the planets were forming from **accretion** (the collision of small planets or **planetesimals**), one of these planets grew at a far faster rate than the others.

▲ Asteroids – Ida is a potato-shaped asteroid with a 'moon' or satellite, Dactyl, seen far right. Ida is in the main asteroid belt shown below.

This planet became Jupiter. As Jupiter grew, its gravity affected large planetesimals – some the size of the Earth. A number of the planetesimals were pulled towards Jupiter, and others were flung out of the Solar System.

▶ Asteroids – The asteroid belt lies between Mars and Jupiter. Both planets are shown here for reference purposes.

As they passed through the inner Solar System, the scattered planetesimals began to interfere with the **orbits** of the planets already forming there. As a result, the inner planets and the planetesimals collided. Most were smashed into fragments by the collisions, but their remains still orbit the **Sun** as the asteroid belt, occasionally colliding with each other and breaking into more fragments.

Some asteroids were big enough to begin to heat up as a result of the collisions, just like Earth, and in these cases the rocks melted, iron sank to the core and molten lava flowed out on the surfaces, again, just like Earth.

The largest asteroid, called **Ceres**, is over 1,000km across. It is thought that there may be half a million asteroids with diameters bigger than one kilometre and countless numbers that are smaller. The smallest asteroids are just a few metres across. Together they have a **mass** of about a twentieth of that of the **Moon**. The large asteroids are shaped like a ball, suggesting that they have built up by accretion, while the smaller ones are very irregular.

On average, a house-sized Apollo asteroid hits the Earth every century; the last one burst over Russia in 1908. An asteroid big enough to threaten life on Earth hits the planet only once every 50 million years or so. The last time this happened may have been the cause of dinosaurs becoming extinct on Earth (although many other scientists believe the extinction of the dinosaurs was due to massive volcanic eruptions).

Some of the largest asteroids even have their own **satellites**.

The biggest asteroid fragment that has landed on the Earth's surface in the last few hundred million years produced Meteor Crater in Arizona in the southwestern United States. (*See also:* **Asteroid number**; **Crater**; **Minor planets**.)

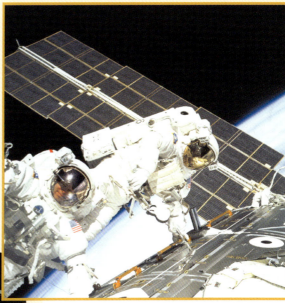

▲ **Astronaut** – An astronaut is a person who travels in space, whether inside a spacecraft or, as here, using a spacesuit to repair equipment in space.

Astronaut
A person who travels in space. The Russian word for astronaut is cosmonaut.

Astronomical unit (AU)
The average distance from the **Earth** to the **Sun**. One AU is 149,597,870 kilometres.

Astronomy
The science of studying space.

Atmosphere
A shell of gas that envelops a planet, moon, or sun. (*See also:* **Atmosphere, the**.)

Atmosphere, the

Surrounding the **Earth** is an invisible 'envelope' of gases known as the atmosphere. Over time these gases have become sorted into layers, each with a different name and different properties.

The main components of the atmosphere are nitrogen (78%) and oxygen (21%). Other important gases are carbon dioxide and water vapour, although together they make up less than 1% of the atmosphere.

The lowest part of the atmosphere contains the water vapour that helps make our clouds and keep our world warm. Above it are layers containing a gas called ozone that shields us from the harmful ultra-violet rays in space. Further out still, there are layers that allow us to send radio waves around the world.

These are the layers of the atmosphere, beginning at the surface: troposphere; stratosphere; mesosphere; thermosphere; and exosphere.

(The **magnetosphere** is not part of the atmosphere, but the region around the Earth affected by the Earth's magnetic attraction.)

▼▶ **Atmosphere** – The atmosphere is the envelope around the Earth that still contains a significant amount of gas. Only the lowest layer, the troposphere, has enough oxygen to support life.

Exosphere (above 600km from the Earth's surface). Air molecules are very rare at these levels, and helium is the most common gas.

Thermosphere (about 500km thick). Extremely thin air. Readily absorbs ultraviolet radiation. Within this layer lies the ionosphere, the place that bounces back medium (MW) and short (SW) radio waves, allowing them to travel large distances around the world.

Mesosphere (about 50km thick). Transparent to the Sun's rays. Temperature decreases with height.

Stratosphere (about 30km thick). The air is very 'thin' but contains important ozone gas. Temperature increases with height.

Troposphere (10–20km thick – thickest over the equator, thinnest at the poles). The layer that contains the clouds. It is mainly transparent to the Sun's rays. The temperature decreases with height.

Aurora

A glow in the ionosphere of a **planet** caused by the interaction between the planet's magnetic field and the **solar wind** (the flow of charged particles from the **Sun**).

The name for the aurora in the highest latitudes of the Northern Hemisphere on Earth is the Aurora Borealis, also called the Northern Lights; the Aurora Australis, or Southern Lights, is a similar effect in the Earth's Southern Hemisphere.

The size of the auroras varies with the amount of solar activity. When the activity is intense, the auroras can be seen from latitudes greater than 40°, but during periods of less activity they may only be visible at above 60°.

Auroras are often a green, white, red, or blue colour. They can look like luminous curtains, arcs and bands, and patches that continually move and change shape. (*See also:* **Magnetosphere**.)

▲ **Aurora** – A typical curtain of light produced where the solar wind comes into the influence of the Earth's magnetic field.

Axis, axes

The centre of rotation of a spinning object. Most **planets** spin counter-clockwise around an axis; only **Venus** spins clockwise. Most axes of rotation are more or less at right angles to the plane of the **orbit**; only **Uranus** has its axes more or less in the plane of its orbit, and so it is described as 'spinning on its back'!

B

Barnard's Star

The second closest **star** to the **Sun**. Some six **light-years** away, it is 2,000 times as bright as the Sun. It is named after E. E. Barnard, who discovered it in 1916.

Beta Centauri

A **binary star**, Beta Centauri or Hadar is the 11th **brightest star** in the night sky. It is about 300 **light-years** from the **Earth**.

Betelgeuse

The common name of the **star** Alpha Orionis. It is the tenth **brightest star** in the sky and is about 1,400 **light-years** away. The star is probably 50,000 times as bright as the **Sun**. Betelgeuse shrinks and swells periodically; and as this happens, it also changes brightness.

Big Bang

One of the most fundamental questions of **astronomy** is how the **Universe** came into being. The 'Big Bang' theory, or model, is the most commonly accepted idea about the evolution of the Universe. According to this theory, the Universe began from a tiny **mass** of material that was unbelievably compressed and unbelievably hot.

The Universe is thought to have begun with a massive expansion of this material between 10 and 12 billion years ago. This is known as the Big Bang, and it might have looked like a fantastic, expanding fireball.

As soon as the Universe began expanding, the material became less dense and much cooler. The first atoms formed within a few seconds of the Big Bang. They were hydrogen, then helium and then lithium.

Some billion years later the Universe was cool enough for other atoms to form. Scientists think that they can detect the remains of the early Universe by looking at the radiation (called background radiation) that is found throughout the Universe.

The Big Bang theory explains how matter and radiation could come about, but it cannot explain why the Big Bang itself came about.

The term Big Bang was coined by Sir Fred **Hoyle** (born 1915).

Binary star

A double **star** that occurs when two stars are so close that they continue to be held close together by their own gravity. Binary stars are very common, making up about half of all known stars.

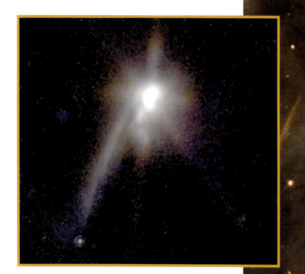

▲ **Binary star** – This NASA Hubble Space Telescope image shows a newborn binary star with a long thin nebula pointing towards a companion object at the bottom left, which could be a planet within another solar system.

Black body

A surface that absorbs all of the energy that it receives from radiation. It appears black because all of the light falling on it is absorbed, and none is reflected.

Black dwarf

A **star** in the last stages of its life. It has collapsed and cooled down so much that it no longer gives out light and so cannot be seen.

Black hole

Stars owe their size to the way they continually use up their fuel. While they remain as fireballs, they can be very large; but when the fuel is finally used up, very large stars will blow up (to form a **supernova**) or collapse inwards (implode). An imploding star becomes denser and denser as its gravity becomes stronger and stronger.

Nobody knows what these bodies look like because the pull of gravity is so great that no light ever leaves them. Black holes are the most mysterious features of the **Universe**.

The centre of a black hole is called a singularity. A star ten times as massive as our **Sun** may collapse into something less than 30km across.

Black holes were predicted by **Einstein's** general theory of relativity. Although they are difficult to see because no light comes from them, they can be detected through the effect their massive gravity fields have on things around them. If one part of a **binary star** (one with two centres) becomes a black hole, it begins to suck matter from the other star, causing it to become so hot that it sends out huge amounts of X-rays. One star in the galaxy Cygnus X-1 is believed to be a black hole.

Some black holes may not be collapsed stars, but a collapse of large masses of interstellar gas (*see:* **Stellar**). The collapse of this matter is unbelievably large and is thought to account for the formation of **quasars**. There is one of these supermassive black holes in the centre of the M87 **galaxy** (*see:* **M**). Its mass is equal to two to three billion **suns**, but it only occupies a space the size of the **Solar System**.

Stars that are less massive than three times our Sun cannot develop enough gravity to become black holes, but instead simply shrink and become **white dwarves** or neutron stars.

Blue giant

A very large **star** that has used up all of the hydrogen fuel in its core and is cooling. The surface temperature of a blue giant is about 30,000°C. When it cools further, it will become a **red giant**.

◀ **Binary star** – Many stars are binary stars, although they might not appear so without the help of a powerful telescope. The large picture shows how stars appear as single points of light; the inset shows how they are typically binaries when seen under high magnification.

Brown dwarf

A body that is too small to have acted like a **star** and to have been fuelled by hydrogen **fusion** in its core, but which is still giving out large amounts of heat. The first brown dwarf was discovered by the **Hubble Space Telescope** in 1995.

C

Callisto

The second largest moon of **Jupiter** and the farthest out of the group called the **Galilean moons** (because they were first described by **Galileo**). It is an icy world about 4,800km across. Its surface reflects little light, so the moon appears darker than the other Galilean moons.

Capella

The common name for Alpha Aurigae, the sixth **brightest star** in the night sky. It appears as a single **star**, but is in fact a **binary star**. It is 41 **light-years** away.

Cassini

A space probe designed to study the **atmosphere** of **Saturn**. It will arrive at Saturn in June 2004. The probe is named after the Cassini family of Italian–French astronomers who lived in the 17th and 18th centuries. The Cassini Division is also the name of a gap in Saturn's rings.

▼ **Cassini** – Launching of the Cassini probe.

▶ **Brightest stars** – The ten brightest stars in order of brightness. Sirius is the very brightest star in the sky (other than the Sun).

Brightest stars

The brightness of a **star** is described by a term called the **stellar magnitude**. The brightest stars are called first-magnitude stars. The next brightest stars are 2.5 times as dim as the first-magnitude stars, and so on. A sixth-magnitude star is about 100 times as dim as a first-magnitude star.

The brightest star in the sky (other than the **Sun**) is **Sirius**. The second brightest is Canopus. Other very bright stars include **Rigel** and **Betelgeuse**. They can be clearly seen with the unaided eye. You can see stars that are fainter than sixth magnitude only by using a telescope.

(*See also:* **Capella** and **Vega**.)

1
Sirius

2
Canopus

3
Rigel Kentaurus

4
Arcturus

5
Vega

6
Capella

7
Rigel

8
Procyon

9
Achernar

10
Betelgeuse

Cassiopeia A

The **brightest star** of the Cassiopeia **constellation** and clearly visible in the night sky. It is about 10,000 **light-years** away and is thought to be the remains of a **supernova**. It is a strong source of radio waves.

Castor

The common name for the **star** Alpha Geminorum, easily seen with the naked eye. It is a multiple star system consisting of two **dwarf binary stars** and two single stars. This group of six stars lies 49 **light-years** away.

Ceres

The first and largest **asteroid** to be discovered (by G. Piazzi in 1801). It is 904km across and contains about a third of the **mass** of the whole asteroid belt.

Chondrite

The most common type of **meteorite**. Its stony structure is mainly made up of tiny ball-like glassy minerals called chondrules.

Chromosphere

The lower part of the solar **atmosphere**, lying between the **photosphere** and the **corona** (*see also:* **Sun, the**).

Cluster of galaxies

Space is not uniformly speckled with **galaxies**. Instead, they lie in patches or clusters. Our local galaxy, the **Milky Way**, is part of one of these clusters known as the **Local Group**. The **Andromeda Galaxy** is another member of this Local Group. Some clusters, such as the one containing Virgo, themselves contain thousands of galaxies.

Coma

The **dust** and gas that surround the nucleus of a **comet**, often teardrop shaped because of the way it is formed by the **solar wind**. The coma only forms when the comet is close to the **Sun**, where the solar wind is strong.

Comet

A small body of ice and rock that orbits the **Sun** – perhaps the remains of the formation of the outer **planets**. They have been likened to huge dirty snowballs. (*See also:* **Kuiper belt**.)

The nucleus of a comet is only a few kilometres across and is invisible for most of its **orbit**. But, as the comet comes within range of the **solar wind**, it develops a spectacular glowing tail that can reach up to 100 million km in length. (*See also:* **Coma**.)

Comets leave a trail of debris behind them as they travel through space. Most of the debris is made up of tiny pieces of rock, or **meteoroids**.

▲ **Comet** – Halley's Comet. The coma forms the 'tail' of the comet.

▼ **Comet** – Comets make very elliptical orbits. Those we see have an orbit that brings them close to the Earth. Encke's Comet and Halley's Comet are shown here as examples.

2010

Dashed red line shows the orbit of Halley's Comet.

Outer blue circle shows the orbit of Uranus

1980

Inner blue circle shows the orbit of Earth.

1985

1986

Dashed purple line shows the orbit of Encke's Comet.

When the **Earth** passes through the path of a comet, the meteoroids crash into the Earth's **atmosphere** as **meteorites** and cause a **meteor** shower as they burn up in the air.

Because the orbits of comets cross that of the Earth, comets are among the most likely bodies to collide with the Earth, and some people believe that collisions in the past may have caused widespread destruction, climate change and the extinction of many species.

Unlike most planets, which have orbits that are roughly circular, the orbits of comets are very elongated, so that they come very close to the Earth for a short while and then speed off into space and are lost from sight for many years.

Because they are so small, many comets are only detected as they come close to the Earth. About ten new comets are spotted each year; and because each one only returns after many tens of years, this means there must be a large number of them speeding through space.

The comet with the shortest orbit is **Encke's Comet**, which returns every 3.3 years. However, those with the longest orbits may only return once in several thousand years. The most famous and brightest comet is **Halley's Comet**, which can be seen every 76 years. The most famous recent comet was **Shoemaker-Levy 9**, which was captured by the world's telescopes as it crashed into the surface of **Jupiter** in 1994 and disrupted the **Jovian atmosphere**.

Conjunction

The time when two bodies in the **Solar System** are in line. The **planets** with **orbits** outside the **Earth** are in conjunction when they lie immediately behind the **Sun**; those with orbits inside the Earth's are in conjunction when they lie both in front of and behind the Sun. Conjunctions also occur between any two other planets and the Earth and also between the Earth, the **Moon** and any other planet.

Constellation

The sky is divided up into 88 regions to allow any star to be found quickly. Each of these regions is called a constellation. They are based on shapes described by the Greek astronomer **Ptolemy** in the 2nd century AD, with later additions. Examples of constellations include Ursa Major, or Great Bear, in the northern sky (its **brightest star** is the Pole Star, **Polaris**) and Crux (the Southern Cross) in the southern sky, which is identified from four bright stars – Alpha, Beta, Gamma and Delta Crusis. (*See also:* **Andromeda**.)

Copernicus

Nicolas Copernicus (1473–1543) was a Polish astronomer and churchman who was the first person to argue against the idea accepted since **Ptolemy** in the 2nd century AD that the **Earth** was the centre of the **Universe**. Instead, he put forward the theory that the Earth spins on its **axis** each day and makes a yearly **orbit** of the **Sun**. He also believed that the Universe stretched out forever.

Copernicus set out a revolutionary idea that would eventually become accepted by all scientists. But, at the time, the Copernican system went against the accepted teaching of the church and so was not made publicly available until the day of his death.

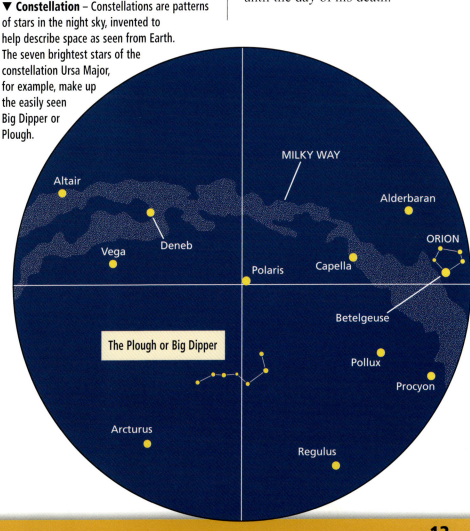

▼ **Constellation** – Constellations are patterns of stars in the night sky, invented to help describe space as seen from Earth. The seven brightest stars of the constellation Ursa Major, for example, make up the easily seen Big Dipper or Plough.

MILKY WAY

Altair

Deneb

Vega

Polaris

Capella

ORION

Alderbaran

Betelgeuse

Pollux

Procyon

Regulus

Arcturus

The Plough or Big Dipper

Corona

The very hot gas (at about two million °C) that stretches out from the surface of the **Sun** in the form of plumes and loops. Material flowing out into space from the corona makes the **solar wind**.

The corona varies with **sunspot** activity.

The corona cannot be seen from the surface of the **Earth** except when the main **disc** of the Sun is blocked out during a total **eclipse**. At these times the corona can be seen as a white **flare** around the solar disc. (*See also:* **Diamond ring** and **Filament**.)

▶ **Corona/Diamond ring** – This is the view that can be seen near the Sun and just at the end of the solar eclipse.

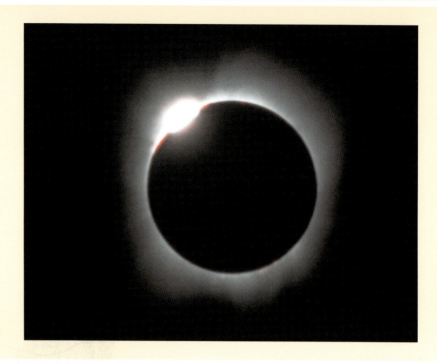

Cosmic rays

Any particles travelling through space at close to the **speed of light**.

Cosmos

Another term for the **Universe**.

Crab Nebula

The remnant of a **supernova** about 7,000 **light-years** away. It is in the **constellation** of Taurus. The Crab Nebula is the remains of a **star** that was seen to explode in 1054 AD.

◀ **Crab Nebula** – At the centre of this spectacular nebula is the Crab Pulsar – the collapsed core of an exploded star. The Crab Pulsar is a rapidly rotating neutron star about 10km across but containing more mass than the Sun. The green, yellow and red colours around the edge are remnants of the star that were sent into space with the explosion.

The inset photo shows a Hubble Space Telescope image of the inner parts of the Crab.

Crater

A depression formed by the impact of a **meteorite**. There are craters on many **planets** and **moons**. Craters are very well preserved on the **Moon** and other planets and moons that have no **atmospheres**. They are less well preserved on the **Earth** because rain and rivers have eroded them. One of the best preserved on Earth is Meteor Crater, in the desert of Arizona.

▶ **Crater** – Inset shows Mimas, a small moon of Saturn that has a very large impact crater compared with its size. If the crater was any larger, it might have destroyed the entire moon.

Crust

The outermost layer of a **planet**. (*See also:* **Earth**.)

D

Deep Space Network (DSN)

A worldwide network of radio telescopes that track space probes. There are three clusters of telescopes: one in the Mojave Desert of California, one near Madrid in Spain and one near Canberra, Australia. The network allows communication with probes in space at all times, even though the **Earth** is spinning.

Deimos

One of the two **moons** of **Mars**.

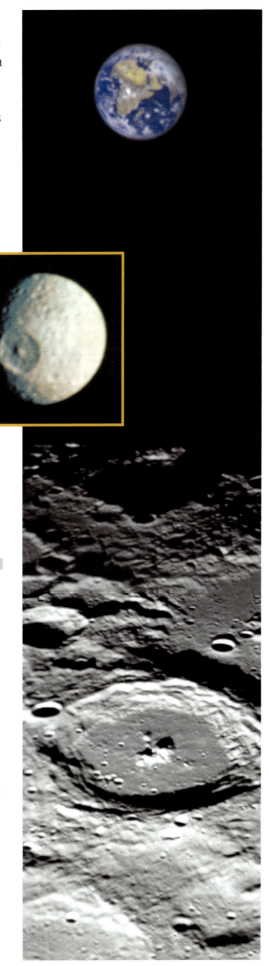

▶ **Crater** – The cratered surface of the Moon.

Deneb

The common name for the **star** Alpha Cygni, a supergiant star some 60,000 times as bright as the **Sun**. It lies about 1,500 **light-years** away and is the farthest bright (**magnitude** 1) star that can be seen with the naked eye. It makes up part of the Summer Triangle of stars.

Diamond ring

The effect seen immediately after a solar **eclipse**, when the first rays of the **Sun** appear like a diamond jewel set against the ring of the **corona**.

Dione

The fourth largest moon of **Saturn**, some 1,120km across. It is probably a rocky moon with an icy surface (*see:* **Moons**).

Disc

The side of a **planet** or **star** that can be seen against the sky.

Dog star

(*See:* **Sirius**.)

Dust

The name given to tiny particles of solid material that occur in space. Dust is thought to make up about 10% of all matter. It is responsible for making distant **stars** look redder and fainter than they otherwise would (just as haze on **Earth** reduces the distance you can see from a hilltop). It is believed that much of the dust contains carbon. It may have formed in the cool, outer regions of **supernovas** and **red giant** stars.

(*See also:* **Accretion** and **Coma**.)

Dwarf star

The name for a small **star** like the **Sun**. Most stars are dwarf stars.

E

Earth

The third **planet** from the **Sun**. It **orbits** between 147,099,590km from the Sun in January and 152,096,150km in July. From space it appears as a small blue planet. It has a diameter of 12,756km and orbits the Sun every 365.25 days.

The Earth has an **atmosphere** made of 78% nitrogen, 21% oxygen and 0.9% argon. There are smaller amounts of carbon dioxide, water vapour, hydrogen and other gases. Because the water vapour changes to water droplets when it makes cloud, the surface of the Earth is often obscured from space.

The Earth is like a ball within a shell within a shell. The innermost part of the Earth is called the core, the shell around it is called the mantle, and it is surrounded by the thin shell that we call the **crust**.

The core and the mantle together make up almost all of the Earth. They are the source of the Earth's magnetism, volcanoes and all of the material that a volcano sends out, and of earthquakes. The crust – the rocks on which we live – is a thin, brittle 'skin' on an Earth scale.

The core

Imagine being squashed under 6,000km of rock. This is exactly what it is like at the centre of the core. The rock around the core acts like a blanket, keeping the heat in – you can start to see why the core is both very hot and why its materials are very compressed.

The centre of the core is a vast liquid ball of white-hot nickel and iron. This inner part of the Earth is a kind of furnace, with the heat trying to get out.

The outer part of the core is not quite so hot and is nearly solid. The heat from the furnace in the centre of the core heats these rocks and makes them move slowly, just as water moves in a pot that is heated on a stove. This kind of movement is called convection.

As the iron rich rocks slowly move around, they create the Earth's magnetism. So, when we use a compass, we are making use of magnetism formed more than 3,000km below our feet!

The mantle

The rock surrounding the core is made mainly of the metals magnesium and iron.

The mantle is about the same distance across as the core – some 3,000km. Most of it is solid, but

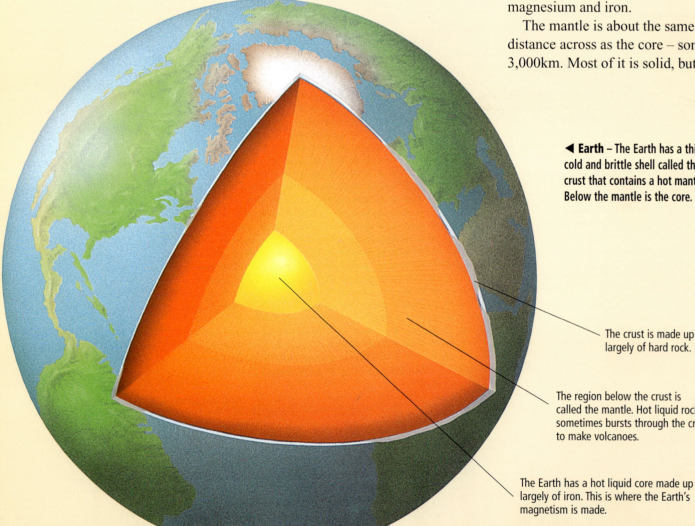

◄ **Earth** – The Earth has a thin, cold and brittle shell called the crust that contains a hot mantle. Below the mantle is the core.

The crust is made up largely of hard rock.

The region below the crust is called the mantle. Hot liquid rock sometimes bursts through the crust to make volcanoes.

The Earth has a hot liquid core made up largely of iron. This is where the Earth's magnetism is made.

▲ **Earth** – The Earth's crust is hard and brittle, and cracks up into giant slabs called plates.

near the top it is almost liquid. It, too, is heated from the core and moves slowly by convection. This convection is responsible for the movement of the crust over the Earth's surface – a process called plate tectonics. The liquid at the top of the mantle is the source of volcanoes.

The crust

The crust is the solid rock on which we live. It is very thin compared with the layers of rock below – something like 25km thick on the ocean floors and 200km thick under the centres of the continents. It is also hard and brittle, which is why it cracks up into giant slabs called plates.

The crust is made from the materials ejected from volcanoes over thousands of millions of years. The ocean floors are made of lava. The lava that was pushed out on land is quickly changed into new materials by weather, rivers, ice and waves.

When the rocks of the mantle move, they drag the thin crust with them, and in time this causes earthquakes and creates mountains and oceans.

(*See also:* **Earth history** and **Earth orbit**.)

Earth history

As far as we can tell, the **Earth** is unique, an accidental mixture of materials that came together in a very special way some 4.6 billion years ago. At first it was nothing more than a dense **mass** of gas, but the force of gravity gradually caused the Earth's materials to collapse inwards, heating the core as they did so. The hot core still drives our world. (*See also:* **Accretion**.)

After about one billion years the surface had cooled and developed a **crust** of solid rocks. At the same time, the surface was bombarded with **meteorites** that made huge **craters** just like those seen on the **Moon** today. Hot rock inside the Earth was continually turned over, dragging the crust apart and allowing vast sheets of molten rock (lava) to flow out and cool to make more crust. This process is still happening today.

As the crust thickened and less lava flowed to the surface, there was an opportunity for gases to condense and form the water in the oceans and the **atmosphere**.

Life forms probably developed first in the hot liquids near volcanic eruptions. Slowly, the developing plant life absorbed carbon dioxide and released oxygen, changing the composition of the air and allowing oxygen-breathing life to colonise the land.

◄ **Earth history** – The earliest Earth collected as a mass of dust and gas that collapsed under the force of gravity. This caused a release of heat that made the planet's rocks melt (**1**). It took a billion years for the surface to cool into a hard crust (**2**). The early Earth was also bombarded by meteorites. In time volcanoes developed and then an atmosphere and oceans (**3**). Life probably developed in the hot liquids near volcanic eruptions. Slowly, the developing plant life helped absorb carbon dioxide and release oxygen, allowing life to colonise the land.

Earth orbit

The path the **Earth** takes around the **Sun**.

The Earth spins on an **axis**, which is an imaginery line drawn between the North Pole and the South Pole. On average the axis tilts 23.5° (degrees) to the plane in which the Earth orbits the Sun, but the angle at which the Earth is tilted relative to the Sun varies. At present it is 21.5°, but over a period of 40,000 years it can become over 3° larger than this. When the Earth tilts more, there are bigger differences between seasons; when the Earth tilts less, the differences between the seasons are smaller.

The Earth also changes its **orbit** around the Sun in a regular way. At times it is almost circular, but over a period of 97,000 years it changes shape until it follows a path like a giant oval (an ellipse). At those times the Earth is cooler in both summer and winter.

These ideas about the Earth's changing movements were used by the Serbian scientist Milutin Milankovitch (1879–1958) to suggest underlying causes for changes in the Earth's climate and for the start of the Ice Ages.

The Earth's magnetic north and south poles are not in the same places as the geographic poles. At present the magnetic poles are at about 76° north, 100° west (in Canada) and 66° south, 139° east (on the Antarctic coast facing Australia).

Eccentric

Another word for elliptical, as in an elliptical (oval) **orbit**.

Eclipse

An eclipse occurs when the normal sunlight received by the **Earth** or the **Moon** is blocked because the paths of the Moon and Earth cross.

Sometimes the Earth blocks out light reaching the Moon, making an eclipse of the Moon; more spectacularly, the Moon blocks out light reaching the Earth, making an eclipse of the **Sun**.

During an eclipse only a small band of the Earth (at most 270km across) experiences total darkness (this area is called an **umbra**). But for people in this small band the sky suddenly darkens and stars become visible.

A much larger band of the Earth's surface experiences partial darkness (an area called the **penumbra**); here people still see a milky white sky.

The Sun's flaring surface, or **corona**, becomes visible only during an eclipse, which is why this event is so important to scientists studying the Sun. (*See also:* **Conjunction**; **Diamond ring**; **Lunar eclipse**.)

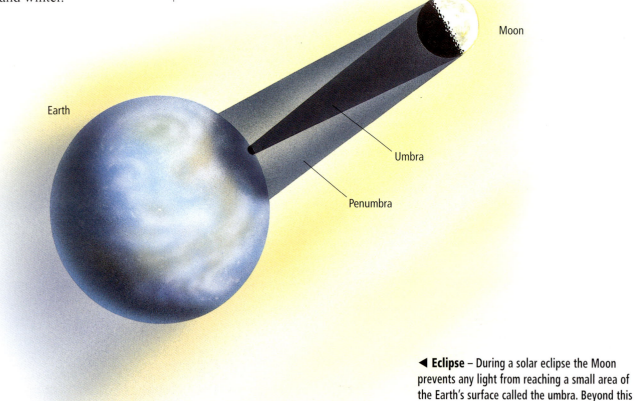

Earth

Moon

Umbra

Penumbra

◄ **Eclipse** – During a solar eclipse the Moon prevents any light from reaching a small area of the Earth's surface called the umbra. Beyond this spot, a large part of the Sun is obscured and people see a partial eclipse. This larger area is called a penumbra.

▶ **Europa** – The surface of Europa which has features resembling ice floes on Earth.

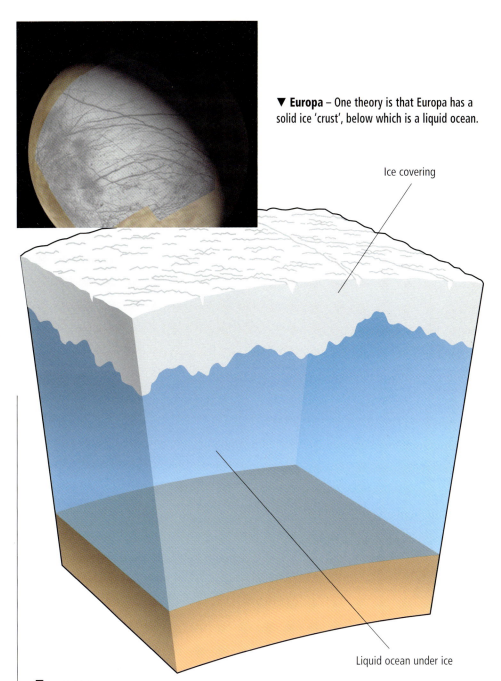

▼ **Europa** – One theory is that Europa has a solid ice 'crust', below which is a liquid ocean.

Ice covering

Liquid ocean under ice

Einstein

Albert Einstein (1879–1955) was born in Germany but became a naturalised Swiss. He was one of the most important scientists of the 20th century, proposing entirely new ways of thinking about space, time and gravitation. Before his time physicists had relied on the laws of motion of Isaac Newton. Although these laws worked well, for many practical reasons they were not suitable for the study of space.

Einstein's theories allow physicists to explain what happens when bodies travel at the **speed of light**. (*See also:* **Black hole**.)

$e=mc^2$ is the fundamental formula of **Einstein's** theory of relativity. Energy (e) is equal to mass (m) multiplied by the **speed of light** squared (c^2). It describes how a small mass travelling very quickly produces an enormous amount of energy.

Encke's Comet

The most frequently appearing **comet**, although it is always faint. It completes its **orbit** in 3.3 years and was named after the German astronomer Johann Franz Enke (1791–1865).

Eta Carinae

A hypergiant **star** that, in 1843, became the second **brightest star** in the sky. It is less luminous now, but is the largest star in the **galaxy**, at 100 times the mass of the **Sun**. It loses about a hundredth of its **mass** each year and is possibly a **supernova**. It is about 8,000 **light-years** away.

Europa

The fourth largest moon of **Jupiter** and the second closest of the four **Galilaen moons**. It is 3,138km across, or approximately the same size as our Moon. It has an icy surface and is believed to be geologically active (*see:* **Moons**).

Evening star

(*See:* **Venus**.)

Expanding Universe

The idea that the **Universe** is getting ever larger, and the **galaxies** are steadily getting farther apart.

The idea of the expanding Universe does not affect small parts of the Universe like the **Solar System** because they are held together by gravity.

Explorer

The name for a series of American spacecraft. Explorer 1 was launched on 31 January, 1958 and was the first successful United States satellite. Scientists used Explorer 1 to discover the **Van Allen belts** around the **Earth**.

▶ **Galaxy** – Most galaxies form a spiral shape. This is NGC4414 as photographed by the Hubble Space Telescope.

F

Filament

A long strand of cool gas suspended in the **Sun's corona**. It looks like a dark line when seen against the corona. It is the same as a **prominence**, except that a prominence appears beyond the corona. Because prominences are seen against the black of space, they appear bright, while the same strands of cool gas seen against the bright corona appear dark. They are connected to the Sun's magnetic field.

Flare

A sudden eruption of energy on the solar **disc**, lasting minutes to hours. The **Sun's** flares throw out massive amounts of particles, adding greatly to the **solar wind**.

Fluorescence

The glowing of a gas when its atoms have been excited by a source of radiation. The radiation may come from a hot **star**. The glow of a **nebula** is due to fluorescence.

Full Moon

The phase of the **Moon** when it lies in the opposite side of the sky from the **Earth**, and thus the full **disc** is illuminated.

Fusion

The process of two atoms joining together. Enormous amounts of energy are released when this happens. Part of this energy is seen in the light from the **Sun** and other **stars**.

G

Galaxy

A giant spiral made up of countless **stars**, gases, **dust** and probably a few **planets**. It is all bound together by gravity in the same way as the planets are bound to the **Sun**.

Galaxies are some of the most obvious features in the **Universe**. Some are small and contain less than a million stars. They are called dwarf galaxies. Others are huge and may contain thousands of millions of stars. They are called supergiants. The largest are 600,000 **light-years** across, meaning that light would take this time just to get from one side to the other.

Galaxies have two shapes: either spiral, with arms, or ovals, without arms. The stars in the oval shapes are more evenly distributed.

Galaxies probably formed from rotating masses of gas early in the life of the Universe. Galaxies do not remain the same, but continually change as the gas remaining in the galaxy condenses into new stars.

We can see the disc part of our galaxy as a shimmering band of stars in the clear night sky. We call this region the **Milky Way**. Some people use the term Milky Way to mean our whole galaxy.

Our galaxy, like others in the Universe, is mainly disc shaped. The rotating disc is 100,000 light-years across and 1,000 light-years thick. The Sun is 26,000 light-years from the centre of our galaxy on one of the outer spiral arms, known as the Orion arm.

Less conspicuous is a sphere surrounding the centre. It contains old stars and makes up just under a third of the **mass** of the galaxy. All of these visible parts of the galaxy are surrounded by invisible dark matter.

The whole of the galaxy contains several million million stars, of which our Sun is an above-average-sized member on one of the outer spiral arms.

Set within the galaxy are stars in many forms of their evolution. Some are new stars set far out on the spiral arms; others, nearer the centre, are up to 14 billion years old; some have even collapsed and produced **black holes**.

Nearby, in astronomical terms, there are 20 large galaxies that together make a cluster. The largest and most prominent of these is called the **Andromeda Galaxy**, more than 2 million light-years away. What we see of this galaxy in the sky is, therefore, what it looked like 2 million years ago!

Many galaxies are visible in the night sky and were classified, along with all other celestial objects, by C. J. Messier in 1771. All of these objects have **M** numbers, such as M31, and this is often how astronauts still refer to them.

Galilean moons

Jupiter's four largest **moons**: **Io**, **Europa**, **Ganymede** and **Callisto**. They were discovered independently by **Galileo** and Marius.

Galileo

A pioneering Italian astronomer, Galileo Galilei (1564–1642) was famous as one of the first people ever to make a telescope. With it he saw what he described as mountains on the **Moon**. He also saw four of the **satellites** of **Jupiter**.

The more Galileo looked at the **Universe** through his telescope, the more he become convinced that the traditional view of the Universe (known and accepted since the time of **Aristotle**) was incorrect. Instead, he believed that Nicolas **Copernicus** held the correct view, and the **Earth** was not the centre of the Universe.

Unlike Copernicus, whose ideas were not published until after his death, Galileo wrote two books that were published during his lifetime. They were unpopular with the church and he was tried for heresy. Galileo was eventually put under house arrest for the rest of his life and forced to say that what he had seen was untrue.

Galileo probe

A space probe launched in 1989 by **NASA** and designed to explore **Jupiter**. Besides photographing the surface, it sent a small probe on a parachute into the **Jovian atmosphere**.

Ganymede

The largest moon of **Jupiter** and one of the **Galilean moons**. It is also the largest moon in the **Solar System**, being 5,262km across. It **orbits** at one million kilometres from the **planet's** surface. It has an icy surface, but also shows signs of past geological activity (*see*: **Moons**).

Gas giants

The name for **Jupiter**, **Saturn**, **Neptune** and **Uranus**. These **planets** contrast with the smaller, **rocky planets** such as the **Earth** and **Mars**.

It is believed that the warmth of the **Sun** boiled many gases off the surface of the rocky planets. But the outer planets are cold worlds, so far from the Sun that they have never lost their light gases. That is why (except for **Pluto**, which is only the size of a **moon**) they are such giant worlds, made of hydrogen and helium gas or frozen water, methane and ammonia.

▼ **Gas giants** – The largest gas giant, Jupiter, seen with its largest moon, Ganymede.

▲ **Ganymede** – (Inset) The surface of Ganymede, showing intriguing signs of geological activity.

Gemini missions

A series of crewed space missions in the earliest days of **NASA's** exploration of space. They were developed in preparation for the **Apollo project**, which would land people on the **Moon**. The crewed flights lasted between March 1965 and November 1966.

Geostationary orbit

An **orbit** about 35,900km above the surface of the **Earth's** equator in which a satellite will move at the same speed as the Earth. As a result, a satellite will always remain in the same place above the equator. This orbit is used for weather and communications satellites.

Giant planet

(*See:* **Gas giants**.)

Giant star

A **star** close to the end of its life that has finished converting its hydrogen into helium and then swollen up. A giant star may be up to 25 times the size of the **Sun** and hundreds of times brighter.

Gibbous

The phase of the **Moon** when it is between half and full illumination. The word gibbous comes from the Latin for hump.

▼ **Gibbous** – More than half illuminated.

▲ **Hale-Bopp Comet**.

Giotto

The first space probe launched by the European Space Agency (ESA). It was launched in 1985 to study **Halley's Comet**. It was later retargeted to study another **comet**.

Goddard Space Flight Center

One of the **NASA** facilities whose tasks include the design and tracking of satellites and the **Hubble Space Telescope**. It is also engaged in space science research.

Great Dark Spot

The large, oval shape on the surface of **Neptune**. It was about 10,000km across and visible when the **Voyager** probe reached Neptune in 1989. It may be a weather feature, a kind of giant storm, like the Great Red Spot of **Jupiter**. Pictures from the **Hubble Space Telescope** no longer show this spot, suggesting that the spots on Neptune come and go more rapidly than those on Jupiter.

Guide star

A **star** that is easy to find with a telescope, and that is close to the part of the **Universe** under observation. The use of guide stars allows faint stars to be found quickly.

H

Hale-Bopp Comet

A **comet** named after the two astronomers who discovered it in 1995. It became prominent in the sky during the second half of the 1990s.

Halley, Edmond

An English astronomer, Edmond Halley (1656–1742) was the first person to map the **stars** in the southern sky. He also predicted that a **comet** he had seen in 1682 would return in 1758. When it did, it was named **Halley's Comet**.

Halley's Comet

The most famous **comet**, named after the astronomer **Halley**, who predicted the return of one of the most spectacular comets to pass close to the **Earth**. It has a return cycle of 76 years.

Halley's Comet has reappeared only 20 times since it was first observed in 239 BC. It last appeared in 1986, when it was inspected by several space probes, including **Giotto**. It will reappear in 2062.

Hawking, Stephen

One of the most famous of modern scientists, Stephen Hawking (born 1942) developed the theories of **Einstein** and others to try to explain such things as **black holes**. In 1988 he wrote the popular science book *A Brief History of Time*, which is about the development of the **Universe**. This book has sold more copies than any other science book.

Helene

One of **Saturn's moons**, sharing the same **orbit** as the moon **Dione**. It is a tiny world less than 40km across. It was discovered by the **Voyager 1** probe in 1980.

Heliosphere

The region around the **Sun** in which the **solar wind** blows.

Helium star

The core of a once massive **star**. It has collapsed to produce a **supernova** explosion.

Herschel, Caroline

The first well-known woman astronomer. Born in Germany, Caroline Herschel (1750–1848) moved to England to help her brother produce a new precision telescope. She discovered several **comets** and **nebulae.**

Herschel, (Frederik) William

Born in Germany (Frederik) William Herschel (1738–1822) lived in England. He was famous for observations made with his own design of telescopes. They were developed with his sister **Caroline**. In 1781 he discovered **Uranus**.

He later built the world's largest telescope up to that time. With it he was able to discover many **binary stars** and **nebulae**. He was the first to realise that our **galaxy** was a flattened disc. He discovered that stars emit infra-red radiation, an important property used today to help map stars.

Hoyle, Sir Fred

An English astronomer (born 1915) who put forward a theory of a steady state **Universe** in which the same amount of matter was continually being created as destroyed. This theory challenged the **Big Bang** theory, but was eventually discarded in favour of the Big Bang. Hoyle actually coined the term 'Big Bang'. He has written many popular **astronomy** and science fiction books.

Hubble, Edwin

Edwin Hubble (1889–1953) was an American astronomer who specialised in studying **galaxies**, and who laid the foundations for their classification. Hubble also studied the speed at which the **Universe** is expanding. The **Hubble Space Telescope** is named after him.

Hubble Space Telescope (HST)

A reflecting telescope built by **NASA** and ESA (the European Space Agency) and launched in 1990 to allow better observation of distant **galaxies**. It orbits 600km above the **Earth's** surface.

◄ Hubble Space Telescope (HST) – Originally sent into orbit with faulty optics, but now corrected and sending back spectacularly clear pictures of deep space.

Hyperion

One of the **moons** of **Saturn**, nearly 1.5 million km from the **planet's** surface. It is about 400km across.

I

Iapetus

The third largest **moon** of **Saturn**, being 1,460km across. It orbits at 5.5 million miles from the surface of the **planet**.

Impact crater

(*See:* **Crater**.)

Inferior planets

The two **planets** closer to the **Sun** than the **Earth** – **Mercury** and **Venus**.

International Space Station (ISS)

A collaborative effort among **NASA**, ESA (European Space Agency) and Russia to build the largest space station ever. The programme is ongoing.

▲ **International Space Station.**

▼▲ **Io** – Io is one of the most geologically active moons in the Solar System. The inset picture shows some of the spectacular volcanoes. In the main picture the surface has pastel colours, and the black, brown, green, orange and red patches show the volcanic areas.

Io

The third largest of **Jupiter's moons**, some 3,630km across. It is the innermost of the **Galilean moons** and orbits at 422,000km from Jupiter's surface. It is geologically very active and has spectacularly explosive volcanoes. The material rising from the volcanoes can reach 280km above the surface and spread out 500km.

J

Janus

A moon of **Saturn** some 200km across and 151,00km from the **planet's** surface (*see:* **Moons**).

Jet Propulsion Laboratory (JPL)

A **NASA** facility in Pasadena, California, that tracks and controls space probes.

Johnson Space Center (JSC)

A **NASA** facility near Houston, Texas, that designs and develops crewed spacecraft. It houses Mission Control for the **Space Shuttle** flights.

Jovian

Anything relating to the planet **Jupiter**.

Jovian planet

Any of the four, outer gaseous **planets**: **Jupiter**, **Saturn**, **Uranus** and **Neptune**. They are also called **gas giants**.

Jupiter

The fifth **planet** from the **Sun** is the planetary giant, over 300 times the **mass** and 1,000 times the volume of the **Earth**. It has a mass two and a half times more than all of the other planets in the **Solar System** combined.

It is, like the Sun, mainly made of nine-tenths hydrogen and one-tenth helium. If it were much bigger, the gravity of the planet would pull the gases together and turn it into a star. It radiates twice as much heat as it gets from the Sun. Jupiter, some 780 million km from the Sun, rotates once every 10 hours, but orbits the Sun only once every 12 years.

Jupiter began as a small rocky planet two or three times the mass of the Earth. That was enough to hold a huge **atmosphere** and to compress the gases near the surface into a liquid. Today, the planet still has a small rocky core, surrounded by thick layers of metallic and liquid hydrogen and helium, which merge into the 'atmosphere' of hydrogen and helium. Jupiter also has an enormously powerful magnetic field.

The atmosphere has winds and clouds that flow in streams parallel to the equator; they correspond to the broad coloured bands that can be seen with a telescope.

The dark bands on the surface are places where gases in the atmosphere are plummeting down to the surface, while the light-coloured bands are places where the gases in the atmosphere are rising. The Great Red Spot is a storm bigger than the Earth. It is a very long-lasting feature

▲ **Jupiter** – The largest of the planets; this view shows the Great Red Spot near the bottom left.

of the atmosphere and has been observed since 1831.

Jupiter has 16 known **moons**. The four brightest are called the **Galilean moons** and are bright enough to be seen with binoculars. (*See also:* **Adrastra**; **Callisto**; **Europa**; **Galileo probe**; **Ganymede**; **Io**; **Voyager**.)

◄ **Jupiter/Io** – Io shown orbiting Jupiter. Notice the wave-like shapes on Jupiter. They are formed by bands of clouds racing in opposite directions.

K

Kelvin (K)

A measurement of absolute temperature. Zero K is called absolute zero and is only approached in deep space; ice melts at 273K (0°C); water boils at 373K (100°C). Named after British scientist Lord Kelvin (1824–1907).

Kennedy Space Center (KSC)

A **NASA** facility at Cape Canaveral, Florida, responsible for launching spacecraft.

Kepler, Johannes

A German astronomer (1571–1630) and the first person to calculate the **orbit** of **Mars** and to find that **planets** move in elliptical (oval) orbits. He developed three laws that tried to explain the way that planets moved. The first law states that the planets move in an ellipse, with the **Sun** at one focus of the ellipse. The second law shows how the speed of a planet must vary, being fastest at the ends of the ellipse – **perihelion** – and slowest near the centre – aphelion (*see:* **Apse**). The third law relates the distances of the planets from the Sun and the time it takes them to orbit the Sun.

Kuiper belt

A belt of 'dirty snowballs' in the outer region of the **Solar System**. It may contain ten million million million 'snowballs'. It is believed to be the source of **comets**.

L

Light-year

The distance light travels in a year at the rate of nearly 300,000 kilometres per second; one light-year is equivalent to 9,460,000,000,000km, or 63,240 AU (**astronomical units**).

In AD 1054 the **Crab Nebula** (7,000 light-years away) was seen to explode, although, in reality, it had exploded 7,000 years before – the light from the explosion had taken all that time to reach **Earth**.

Local group

The group or **cluster of galaxies** that contains our galaxy. It contains 31 galaxies. The closest to us is the **Andromeda Galaxy**.

Luna

The name for a series of spectacularly successful Soviet probes launched at the **Moon**. Luna 1, launched in 1959, was the first space probe ever, and Luna 2 (also 1959) was the first artificial object to reach another body in space. Luna 3 (also 1959) took the first pictures of the far side of the Moon. Luna 9 (1966) made the first soft landing on the Moon and sent back the first pictures from its surface.

Lunar eclipse

An **eclipse** that occurs when the **Moon** passes through the **Earth's** shadow.

Lunar module

The name of the spacecraft used by the **Apollo project astronauts** to land on the **Moon**. It contained two astronauts, who were the first humans to land on a body in space.

Lunar orbiter

A series of probes that came before the **Apollo project** and were designed to orbit and photograph the **Moon** to find suitable landing sites for the **Lunar module**.

M

M

Short for Messier object. In 1771 C. J. Messier catalogued all of the celestial objects he could see. Each was given a number (for example, M31). It was later discovered that some were **galaxies**, some **stars** and some were **nebulae**. The M numbering system is still widely used because it is a good shorthand description for the most prominent objects in the night sky.

Magellan

A **NASA** space probe designed to investigate **Venus**. It photographed the entire surface using radar. The probe later burned up in the Venusian **atmosphere**.

▼ Kennedy Space Center – Main centre for the launch of the Space Shuttle and other spacecraft.

Magnetosphere

A giant invisible shell beyond the **Earth's atmosphere**. It reaches about ten Earth diameters forward of the Earth and several thousand Earth diameters back into space, forming a tail.

The magnetosphere does not contain any air from the Earth, but it is where the magnetism from the Earth reaches out into the **solar wind**. The power produced in this region is about 100 billion watts, and part of that power produces the night-time displays called **auroras**.

The magnetotail is the portion of a planetary magnetosphere that is pushed in the direction of the solar wind.

▼ **Magnetosphere** – This cross-section shows the way the magnetosphere is buffeted by the solar wind. The result is to squash the magnetosphere in the direction of the solar wind and to produce a long tail in the 'lee' of the Earth.

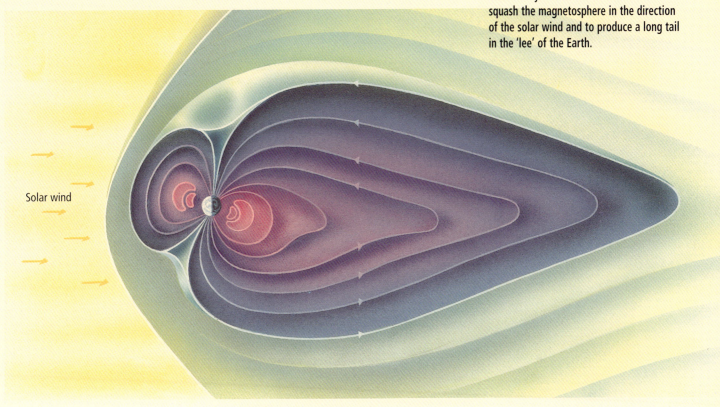

Solar wind

Magnitude

The degree of brightness of a body in space. Magnitude was first used by the Ancient Greeks. They named the bright **stars** that were first seen in the evening sky as magnitude 1. They then defined less bright stars in steps as the sky darkened further, until magnitude 6 was allocated to stars that could only be seen with the naked eye in a totally dark sky.

Since that time the scale has been redefined. The **brightest star** has a magnitude of –1.4, and the faintest visible star has a magnitude of 6. The scale is organised so that a decrease of one unit represents an increase in apparent brightness by a factor of about 2.5.

Mare

Latin word for sea. **Galileo** thought the dark areas on the **Moon** were seas. We now know the Moon is completely dry, but the name is still used for the flat, featureless areas of the Moon.

◀ **Mare** – Mare Tranquillitatis (Sea of Tranquillity) is the large, dark area near the centre of the photograph. Apollo 11 landed here on 20 July, 1969.

Mariner

A series of early **NASA** space probes. Mariner 2 (1962) was the first probe to reach another **planet** (**Venus**). Mariner 4 (1964) gave the first close-up views of **Mars**, and Mariner 9 (1971) was the first probe to go into orbit around another planet (Mars). Mariner 10 (1973) was the first probe to visit more than one planet (Venus and **Mercury**).

Mars

Mars (diameter 6,800km) is the fourth **planet** from the **Sun**. About a tenth of the **mass** of the **Earth**, Mars has a thin **atmosphere** rich in carbon dioxide. It is 95% carbon dioxide, nearly 3% nitrogen and nearly 2% argon. Free oxygen makes up only 0.1%. The dry, volcanic rocky surface is made of basalt, the same rock that covers much of the Earth. When it weathers, the iron in it turns rusty red. **Dust** storms are common and may cover the entire planet for weeks. This makes the planet look red when seen in the night sky.

Mars has two small moons, Phobos and Deimos. Mars spins on its **axis** at about the same rate as the Earth and orbits 240 million km from the Sun. Mars appears to have strange features on its surface called canals, which led people in the past to wonder if there had ever been life on the planet. Some 'canals' are, in fact, rift valleys, signs of the way the surface formed (*see:* **Valles Marineris**). Others may well be dried-up canyons that were cut by rivers several hundred million years ago. But they are mainly optical illusions. Only ice now exists on Mars.

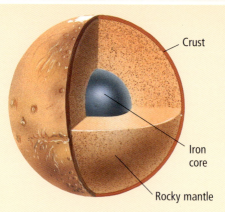

▲ **Mars** – The structure of Mars. A thin crust surrounds a thick mantle, which, in turn, encloses a small core.

Crust

Iron core

Rocky mantle

▲ **Mars** – A piece of Mars that landed in Antarctica as a meteorite. It gave vital clues to the nature of the red planet.

Mars is a geologically active world. Volcanoes grow to spectacular heights on Mars: The largest yet spotted – Olympus **Mons** – is 24km high and 500km across its base, three times the height and four times the breadth of the largest volcano on Earth. Mars has polar ice caps like Earth, but on Mars they grow and shrink dramatically each year as the seasons change, mainly due to sheets of frozen carbon dioxide.

Mars has no magnetic field. (*See also:* **Mariner**.)

▼ **Mars** – The Martian surface as seen from Viking Lander 2. The surface is mostly dust or sand with some large rocks. It looks not unlike a desert on Earth.

Mass

A way of describing the amount of matter in something. The mass of an object gives rise to its gravitational force. The gravitational force created by its mass gives an object its **weight**. Objects in space are often weightless, meaning they are not acted on by any significant external gravitational force, but they still have mass.

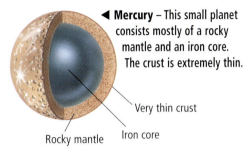

◄ **Mercury** – This small planet consists mostly of a rocky mantle and an iron core. The crust is extremely thin.

Very thin crust

Rocky mantle   Iron core

Mercury

Mercury (diameter 4,900km) is the closest **planet** to the **Sun**. It follows the most elliptical (oval) path of all the planets except **Pluto**. It appears grey in telescopes and has a reflectivity similar to the **Moon** (*see:* **Albedo**).

Because its path keeps it close to the Sun, it is difficult to see Mercury with the naked eye. Mercury has just a trace of **atmosphere** – mainly made up of sodium, helium and hydrogen. It has a cratered surface (*see:* **Crater**).

Without a significant atmosphere, its surface temperature changes violently each day. The temperature soars to over 470°C by day, nearly five times the boiling point of water, but plummets to −183°C at night.

Mercury is just under half the diameter of the **Earth** and has a large iron core, possibly molten, responsible for weak magnetic fields. The planet orbits the Sun at about 60 million km once every 88 days and spins on its **axis** once every 58 days. (*See also:* **Mariner**.)

Mercury project

The first **NASA** project to send people into space. The first American sent into orbit was John Glenn, in 1962.

Meteor

A brief streak of light seen when a **meteoroid** enters the **atmosphere**. It is commonly called a **shooting star**.

Meteoroid

A small rock in space, often no more than a few centimetres across. The majority of them are fragments of **asteroids**, but others come from sources scattered randomly in space. Because they mostly come from asteroids, they are made of mixtures of rock, carbon and water (dirty snowballs). They cross the **orbit** of the **Earth** all the time and can be seen burning up in the Earth's **atmosphere** at night, making the faint streaks of light called **shooting stars**. The larger meteoroids sometimes reach the Earth before they burn up completely (*see:* **Meteorite**).

Meteoroids are the oldest known rocks, with an average age of 4.6 billion years. Their age is one reason why scientists suggest a similar age for the Earth and the **Solar System**.

Meteorite

A piece of a **meteoroid** that survives the trip through the **Earth's atmosphere** and hits the surface of the Earth. The most famous of them formed Meteor Crater in Arizona. (*See also:* **Chondrite** and **Crater**.)

Milky Way

The band of shimmery **stars** and glowing gas that is seen across the sky on a clear night. It marks the disc region of our **galaxy**.

Minor planets

Another term used for **asteroids**.

Mir

A Soviet (Russian) space station launched in 1986 and crewed continuously until 2000. It was the longest surviving manned orbiting spacecraft. From 1995 it was operated with the co-operation of **NASA** and was visited by the **Space Shuttle**.

Miranda

The fifth largest moon of **Uranus** (*see:* **Moons**), some 480km across and 130,000km from the **planet's** surface. It is an extraordinary place, made up of very different types of geological activity. It so resembles a patchwork of different worlds that scientists believe it formed from a giant collision that first blew it apart before most of the parts were pulled together again by gravity.

Mons

The Greek word for mountain, for example, Olympus Mons on **Mars**.

▼ **Mons** – Spectacular Olympus Mons is the largest volcano in the Solar System. It has a summit 24km above the surrounding plains.

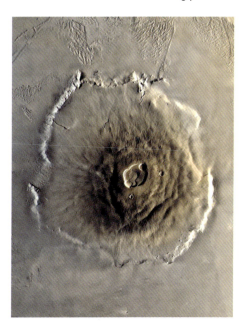

Moon, the

The Moon (diameter 3,476km) is a natural **satellite** of the **Earth** and fifth largest moon in the **Solar System** (*see:* **Moons**).

The Moon appears to be almost trapped in time. While we are used to the surface of the Earth changing, nothing has changed on the Moon for perhaps thousands of millions of years. In this time some of the continents on the Earth's surface have travelled half-way around the world!

The Moon and Earth orbit together in such a way that we only see 59% of the Moon's surface: Before spacecraft were sent to photograph the 'dark side' of the Moon in 1959, nobody had any idea what the far side looked like. (*See also:* **Apollo project**; **Luna**; **Lunar module**; **Lunar orbiter**; **Pioneer**; **Surveyor**.)

The Moon's orbit

The Moon is about one-eightieth the **mass** of the Earth. The Moon and the Earth move together like a double **planet**. The Moon is tilted by just over 5° to the plane in which the Earth moves around the **Sun**. This oval-shaped **orbit** takes the Moon as far away from the Earth as 407,000km and brings it as close as 356,000km.

The near side of the Moon

The Moon's surface is covered with large **craters**. Many are incredibly old, perhaps over three and a half billion years old. When the **meteorites** that caused these

▶ **Moon** – Astronauts exploring one of the rocky parts of the Moon's surface.

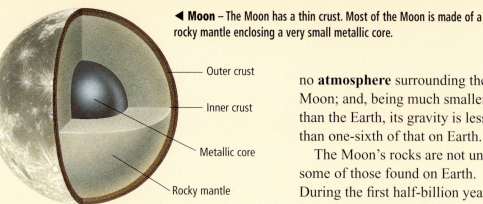

◀ **Moon** – The Moon has a thin crust. Most of the Moon is made of a rocky mantle enclosing a very small metallic core.

Outer crust

Inner crust

Metallic core

Rocky mantle

craters hit the Moon, there was still no life on Earth, and oceans were only just forming. The Moon has not changed since that time.

The Moon's surface and structure

Although there is no life on the Moon, it has a structure made up of layers similar to those of the Earth. The core, however, is solid rock, which is why the Moon has no magnetic field, and which is why the surface never suffers earthquakes. Moreover, there is

Sea of Tranquillity

no **atmosphere** surrounding the Moon; and, being much smaller than the Earth, its gravity is less than one-sixth of that on Earth.

The Moon's rocks are not unlike some of those found on Earth. During the first half-billion years of the Moon's history it was still hot enough for volcanoes to produce great lava flows. However, since then it has cooled, and all activity has died away. As a result there are no overturning movements – the reason the surface has been left undisturbed for so long.

There are two types of landscape on the Moon – a rough, bright mountainous land that covers the majority of the surface, and a darker, flatter land that occupies less than a third of the surface. Early astronomers thought of them as 'continents' and 'oceans', which is why the flat areas – even though they are totally dry – are called 'seas' and 'oceans' on lunar maps (*see:* **Mare**).

Craters cover the Moon's surface. The largest (like the Sea

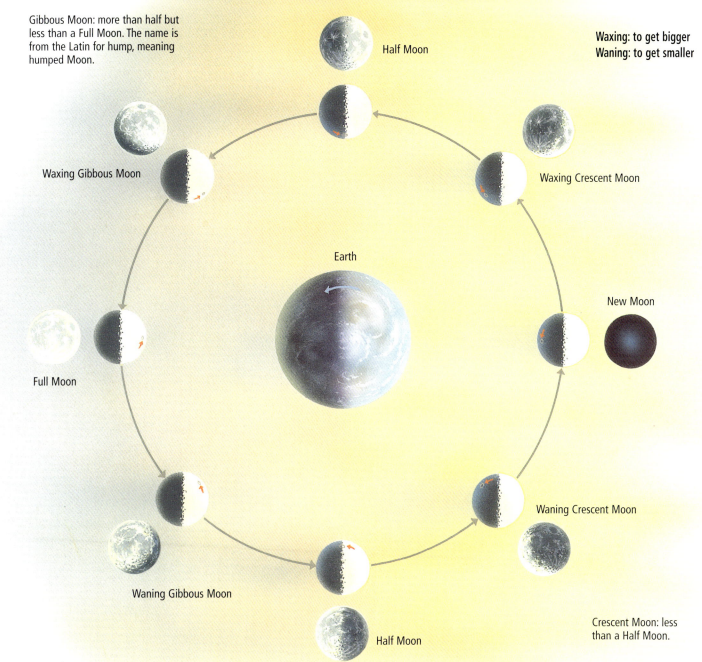

Gibbous Moon: more than half but less than a Full Moon. The name is from the Latin for hump, meaning humped Moon.

Half Moon

Waxing: to get bigger
Waning: to get smaller

Waxing Gibbous Moon

Waxing Crescent Moon

Earth

New Moon

Full Moon

Waning Crescent Moon

Waning Gibbous Moon

Half Moon

Crescent Moon: less than a Half Moon.

Sunlight

▲ **Moon, phases** – The phases of the Moon.

of Rains) are over 1,000km across. They were formed during the early history of the Moon, when meteorites struck the unprotected surface. The impact of the larger meteorites would have generated so much heat that the rock would have become molten and flooded over the land, producing areas with a smooth surface.

The Moon may have been formed when a large object struck the still-forming Earth, tearing a chunk of rock away.

Moon, phases

Neither the **Earth** nor the **Moon** has any light of its own. But as they orbit the **Sun**, they are illuminated by light from it. The way we see this illumination creates the phases of the Moon.

The Moon revolves around the Earth in 27 days, 7 hours, 43 minutes and 11.6 seconds. This is called a sidereal month. However, because the Earth is also moving around the Sun, the time it takes

for the Moon to make a complete orbit and return to the same phase (i.e. have the same illumination when seen from the Earth) is a little longer – 29 days, 12 hours, 44 minutes and 2.8 seconds.

A **gibbous** Moon occurs when the Moon is between half and a **full Moon**. The crescent Moon is less than half a moon.
(*See also:* **Lunar eclipse**.)

Moons (satellites)

Astronomers call any small body that orbits a **planet** a satellite. The **Moon** is a very large satellite 'captured' by the **Earth's** gravity. Most other planets have much smaller satellites, or moons. The outer planets have so many satellites they are called swarms. The four largest satellites that orbit **Jupiter** are each the size of our Moon. The largest moon orbiting **Saturn** (called **Titan**) is bigger than the planet **Mercury** and even has its own **atmosphere**. (*See also:* **Shepherd moon**.)
(*For more individual moons see:*
Adrastra; **Ariel**; **Callisto**; **Deimos**; **Dione**; **Europa**; **Ganymede**; **Helene**; **Hyperion**; **Iapetus**; **Io**; **Janus**; **Miranda**; **Phobos**; **Triton**.)

Morning star

(*See:* **Venus**.)

N

NASA

The National Aeronautics and Space Administration is a United States government agency founded in 1958 to focus research on aircraft and space. It is more famous for its space flights. Its headquarters are in Washington, DC, but it has many facilities around the USA, including the **Jet Propulsion Laboratory**, **Kennedy Space Center** and the **Goddard Space Flight Center**.

Nebula, nebulae

A diffuse **mass** of interstellar **dust** and gas (*see:* **Stellar**).

▶ **Nebula, nebulae** – The Ant Nebula (Menzel 3). This is a picture of fiery lobes spreading out from a dying, sun-like star. This may be what our Sun will look like in its dying stages too.

Neptune

Neptune (diameter 49,500km) is the eighth **planet** and the farthest of the **gas giants** from the **Sun**, orbiting at 4.4 billion km from it, with a rotation of 165 years and a spin of 16 hours.

It is about 17 times the **mass** of the **Earth**. Like **Uranus**, Neptune's **atmosphere** is made of hydrogen and helium. Because it has a large magnetic field, it is thought the planet has a molten rocky core. The surface is very cold, –220°C, yet it would be even colder if there were not a source of heat from the core. A system of **dust** rings surrounds the planet.

The surface atmosphere has dark rings and spots like those on **Jupiter**. One prominent feature for many years was the **Great Dark Spot**.

(*See also:* **Triton** and **Voyager**)

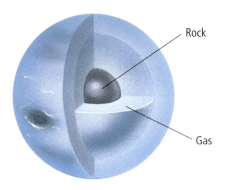

Rock

Gas

▲ **Neptune** – Neptune has a very thick hydrogen-helium atmosphere, then a liquid 'mantle' of water, helium and hydrogen, and possibly a molten rocky core.

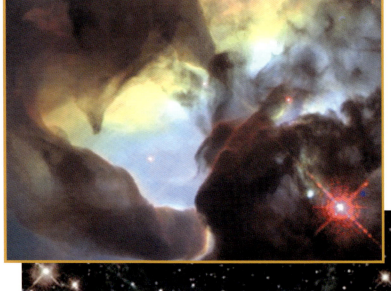

◀ **Nebula, nebulae** – The Laguna Nebula.

North Star

(*See:* **Polaris**.)

Nova

A nova is a **binary star** in which the **stars** interact to release enormous amounts of energy in an unpredictable way.

O

Omega Centauri

The brightest cluster of **stars** in the sky. It may contain millions of old stars.

Orbit

The path of an object that is moving around a second object or point.

Everything in the **Universe** contains a pull, or a force, we call gravity. The bigger the body, the bigger the force of gravity it has. The **Moon** is only one-eighth the **mass** of **Earth**, and so it has one-eighth the pull of Earth's gravity. The **Sun** is big enough for its pull of gravity to spread out all the way to **Pluto**, some 6 billion km.

Gravity would pull the **planets** and their **moons** into the Sun if they were not moving in curved – circular or elliptical (oval) – paths, or orbits. The orbits throw the planets away from the Sun and thus balance out the pull from the Sun. The orbit of the Earth around the Sun takes about 365 days to complete (actually 365.25, so that every four years there is one extra day – the leap year).

The Moon would be pulled into the Earth if it, too, were not in a curved orbit. The Moon orbits the Earth once every 28 days. This is called a lunar month. (See also: **Apse**; **Earth orbit**; **Geostationary orbit**; **Precession**.)

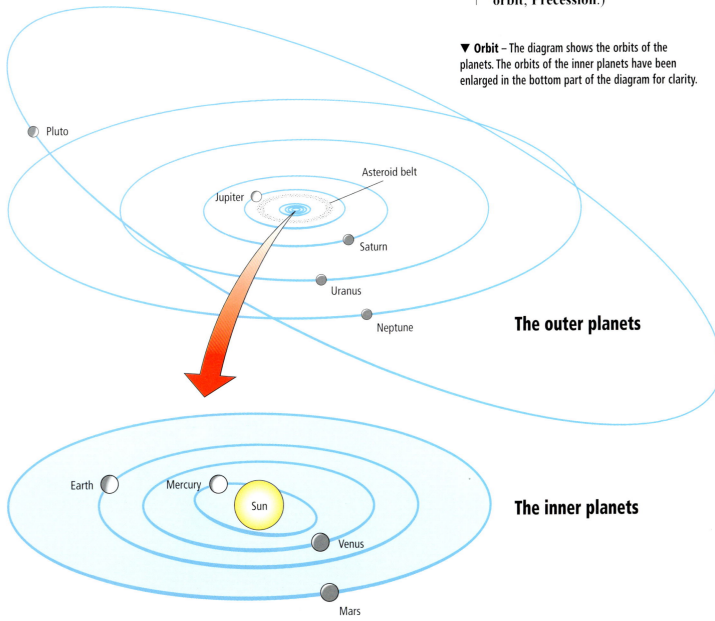

▼ **Orbit** – The diagram shows the orbits of the planets. The orbits of the inner planets have been enlarged in the bottom part of the diagram for clarity.

Pluto

Asteroid belt

Jupiter

Saturn

Uranus

Neptune

The outer planets

Earth   Mercury

Sun

The inner planets

Venus

Mars

P

Parsec

A unit of distance in space. It is equal to 3.26 **light-years**.

Penumbra

The outer region of the shadow cast during an **eclipse**, producing a partial eclipse.

Periapsis

The point in an **orbit** closest to the **planet**. (*See also:* **Apse**.)

Perigee

The point in an **orbit** closest to the **Earth**.

Perihelion

The point in an **orbit** at which a **planet** is closest to the **Sun**.

Phobos

One of the two **moons** of **Mars**.

Photosphere

The visible surface of the **Sun** or any other **star**. The convectional rising and falling of hot gases in the photosphere makes the surface look like grains of rice.

Pioneer

A series of **NASA** space probes that began in 1958 to study the **Moon**. The last ones were sent to look at the distant **planets** and provide information about their environment before the **Voyager** probes were launched. Most of these probes are currently heading out into deep space.

Planet

A body in space that does not give out light and that orbits a **star**. There is no hard-and-fast rule about how small a planet can be; **Pluto** is only a little bigger than some asteroids, also known as **minor planets**. (*See also:* **Earth**; **Mars**; **Jupiter**; **Mercury**; **Neptune**; **Saturn**; **Uranus**; **Venus**.)

Planetesimal

A small rocky **mass** less than 100km across that was one of a vast number that formed in the early stages of the **Solar System**. As planetesimals came together (by **accretion**), they formed **planets**.

Plasma

A low-density gas that contains charged atoms.

Pluto

Pluto (diameter 2,300km) is the ninth **planet** from the **Sun**. Pluto orbits the Sun once every 248 years at a distance of 5.9 billion km, marking the very edge of the **Solar System**.

It is the smallest planet and quite unlike the neighbouring **gas giant** planets. Some scientists think it is really no more than a large **asteroid**. Because of its distance from the **Earth** and its small size, it was not discovered until 1930.

Pluto is a frozen world with an **atmosphere** of methane gas enveloping a cold rocky or possibly ice core. (*See also:* **Voyager**.)

Polaris, Pole star

The North Pole star, also called Alpha Ursa Minoris. It is a supergiant star 820 **light-years** from the **Earth**. It lies about 1° above the geographical North Pole. The South Pole star is Sigma Octanis.

Precession

The wobbling motion of a body as it follows its **orbit**. The **Earth** wobbles as a result of the combined gravitational effects of the **Sun**, **Moon** and other **planets**.

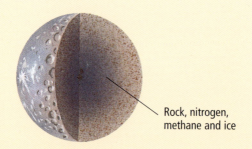

Rock, nitrogen, methane and ice

▲ Pluto is so small and distant that little is known about it for certain.

▼ Pluto on the left and its moon Charon on the right, taken by NASA's Hubble Space Telescope. Pluto was 2.6 billion miles away from Earth when this image was taken. Charon was not discovered until 1978.

Prominence

An eruption of hot gases beyond the **photosphere** seen as a dark area in the **corona** of the **Sun**.

▼ **Prominence** – Solar prominences are some of the most spectacular sights in the Solar System. The one shown here leaps half the radius of the Sun, following a magnetic line of force.

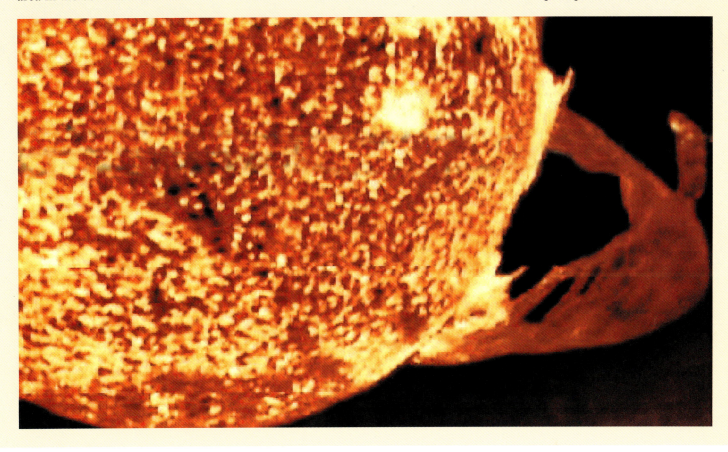

Ptolemy

Claudius Ptolemaeus was a Greek scientist who lived in Alexandria, Egypt, in the 2nd century AD. Although almost nothing is known of his life, he played an extremely important part in the history of **astronomy** through his book *The Great Astronomer*. In it he set out the thinking of the Ancient Greeks, including one of the earliest astronomers Hipparchus.

He made a star catalogue, extending the 850 stars identified by Hipparchus to 1,022.

Ptolemy wrote down the Greek belief that the **Earth** was the centre of the **Universe** and that all other bodies, including the **stars** and our **Sun**, revolved around it. This became known as the Ptolemaic System and was accepted for nearly 1,500 years. Ptolemy believed that, because everything fell to the centre of the Universe (as he thought), and because falling objects fall towards the centre of the Earth, the Earth must be at the centre of the Universe.

Ptolemy thought the **Solar System** was organised in this way (starting at the centre and moving outwards): Earth, **Moon**, **Mercury**, **Venus**, Sun, **Mars**, **Jupiter** and **Saturn.**

Q

Quasar

A rare, extremely bright object about 100,000 **light-years** across. It releases enormous amounts of radiation, possibly from gas spiralling into a **black hole**.

R

Red dwarf

A cool, faint **star** of small **mass**.

Red giant

A **star** that has low surface temperature and a large diameter relative to the **Sun**.

Rigel

The common name for the star Beta Oriois. It is the seventh **brightest star** in the sky. It is a supergiant star 1,400 **light-years** away and 150,000 times as bright as the **Sun**.

Rocky planets

Although the **planets** that orbit the **Sun** are roughly the same age, they vary greatly in their size and in the materials from which they are made. The **Earth** is one of a group of five planets that are largely made of solid rock. (*See also:* **Mars**; **Mercury**; **Pluto**; **Venus**.)

S

Satellite

A body that revolves around a larger body (*see:* **Moons**).

▲ **Saturn V rocket** – Blasting off from the Kennedy Space Center.

Saturn V rocket

The main launching rocket for many US space probes.

Shepherd moon

A **moon** with gravity that has an important effect on the **dust** and rocks in the rings near it. For example, two shepherd moons – Pandora and Prometheus – contain the F Ring around **Saturn**.

Shoemaker-Levy 9 Comet

A **comet** discovered in 1993 when it was captured by **Jupiter's** gravity. It broke up into several fragments and they plummeted

Saturn

Saturn (diameter 120,500km) is a giant **planet** (**gas giant**) that orbits the **Sun** at a distance of 1.4 billion km once every 29 years. It spins on its **axis** once every 10.6 hours.

It is about a third of the **mass** of **Jupiter** (100 times the mass and nearly 800 times the volume of the **Earth**). It is the only planet with an average density less than that of water.

Saturn has a small rock core surrounded by an enormously thick layer of metallic and liquid hydrogen, which in turn is surrounded by a hydrogen–helium **atmosphere** made up of 96% hydrogen and 4% helium.

Saturn's most striking feature – which can be seen even with a low-power telescope – is the **dust** bands that surround its equator (called the F Ring). There are three main rings and every ring is divided into numerous smaller rings.

Saturn has 18 **moons**, more than any other planet. The largest is **Titan**. (*See also:* **Cassini** and **Voyager**.)

(*For Saturn's moons see:* **Dione**; **Helene**; **Hyperion**; **Iapetus**; **Janus**; **Shepherd moon**.)

Rocky core

Dust bands

Gas

Liquid

▲ **Saturn** – Saturn has an atmosphere of hydrogen and helium. Below is liquid and then metallic hydrogen. At the very centre is a rocky core. Rings of dust and rock surround the planet, the rings being separated by shepherd moons.

into Jupiter's **atmosphere** between 16 and 22 July, 1994. The impacts showed up as dark spots, which then developed into a dark belt. They helped astronomers understand more about the **Jovian** atmosphere.

▲ **Shoemaker–Levy 9 Comet** – The comet's 21 icy fragments stretched across 1.1 million km of space, or three times the distance between Earth and the Moon.

Shooting star

A **meteoroid** burning up in the **Earth's atmosphere**. It is believed that 100 million meteoroids produce shooting stars every day.

Most of them are less than a centimetre across.

Sirius

The common name for the **star** Alpha Ursae Majoris and the **brightest star** in the sky.

Skylab

A **NASA** space station launched in 1973. It was made of the converted upper stage of a **Saturn V rocket**. After it had been used by three space crews, it was allowed to re-enter the **Earth's atmosphere** and burn up.

▲ **Saturn** – Saturn, showing the most prominent rings.

▲ **Saturn** – A Saturnian 'family' picture using images of Saturn and six of its 18 moons. It shows Dione in the foreground with Saturn behind, then Tethys and Mimas to the right, and Enceladus and Rhea off Saturn's rings to the left. Titan is shown farthest away at the top and also in the picture below.

▲ **Saturn** – A close-up of Saturn's clouds.

Solar System

The Solar System is that part of the **Universe** that contains the **Sun** and all the bodies that **orbit** around it.

Scientists believe the Solar System began when a spinning interstellar cloud (*see:* **Stellar**) of gas and **dust** began to collapse. The more it collapsed, the faster it began to spin (just as ice-skaters spin faster when they draw in their arms), and the more it began to flatten. Eventually, it became a rapidly spinning disc with a central ball of very concentrated gas, which later formed into the Sun. The Sun now contains 99.9% of the matter in the Solar System.

The Sun was not able to use up all of the material in the cloud, and so it gradually began to form its own clusters of material. Close to the Sun, where it was relatively hot, **dust** collected to make **rocky planets** like **Earth**. Farther out it was cooler, and that allowed gas as well as dust to accumulate, the gas eventually forming the **atmospheres** around the **gas giants** like **Jupiter**.

As each cluster grew in its own part of the Solar System, its gravity swept most of the surrounding space clear.

It is believed that, during the early formation of the Solar System, there were over 100 planets. However, some of them collided and were absorbed by the biggest planets, while others were smashed into fragments, some of which now remain as the **asteroid** belt.

Some **moons** are believed to have formed as clumps of material

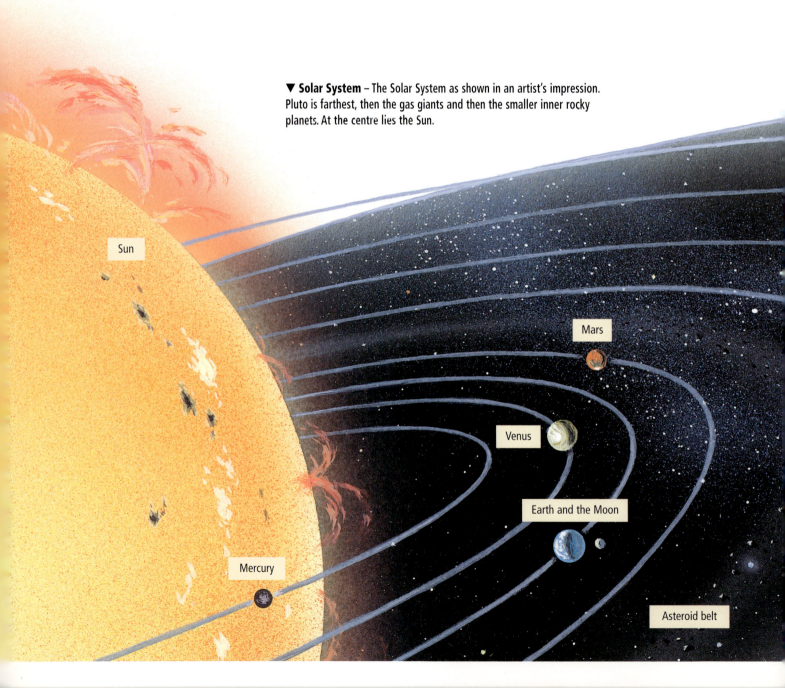

▼ **Solar System** – The Solar System as shown in an artist's impression. Pluto is farthest, then the gas giants and then the smaller inner rocky planets. At the centre lies the Sun.

Sun

Mars

Venus

Earth and the Moon

Mercury

Asteroid belt

just like planets, while others – including our **Moon** – may have been the result of a planet colliding with the Earth and sending debris into space, which then gathered again as a moon.

Giant impacts during the early stages of the Solar System may well have sent some planets careering off on different orbits. This could explain why **Uranus** spins on its back, why **Venus** spins the opposite way from the other planets and why each of the planets has a differently shaped orbit.

Structure

The Solar System contains nine main orbiting worlds called planets, with their 61 moons, all orbiting the Sun. The planets lie far apart from each other, orbiting in different ways and at different speeds and they spin on their **axes** at different rates. The inner planets – **Mercury**, Venus, Earth and **Mars** – are rocky worlds, while most of the outer giant planets – Jupiter, **Saturn**, Uranus and **Neptune** – are mainly made of gases and liquids. **Pluto**, the outermost of the planets, is a small rocky world. The Solar System, however, extends far beyond Pluto. (*See also:* **Kuiper belt**.)

The size of the Solar System

The enormity of the Solar System can be judged by the time a particle of light (a photon) leaving the Sun and travelling at about one billion km an hour, takes to reach each planet. Light from the Sun reaches the nearest planet, Mercury, in just three minutes, flies past the Earth after eight minutes, and takes five and a half hours to reach the outermost planet, Pluto. From Pluto the Sun appears as just a disc of light set in the black starry sky, only a bit brighter than the other stars.

Pluto

Neptune

Jupiter

Uranus

Saturn

Solar wind

The **Sun** is continuously sending out a stream of charged particles into space. As they move through space, they create the solar wind. The **Earth** is always in the path of the solar wind, and the outer layer of the **atmosphere** (the ionosphere) is constantly being battered by it.

The solar wind flows at high speed – between 300 and 700km/s. Just like a boat moving quickly through water, the Earth's passage through the solar wind makes the wind change shape. There is a bow wave facing the Sun and a lee of tail wave behind it. (*See also:* **Magnetosphere**.)

Soyuz

Russian spacecraft designed for three **astronauts** (cosmonauts). The first Soyuz flight was in 1967. It is now used as a shuttle for taking crews or supplies to space stations.

Space Shuttle

A reusable spacecraft built by **NASA** that can be launched like a rocket but which lands under its own power like a plane. It can carry up to eight **astronauts**, together with a large payload in its cargo bay. The first Space Shuttle was launched in 1981. There are four Space Shuttles: Atlantis, Columbia, Discovery and Endeavour. One Space Shuttle, Challenger, exploded and was replaced by Endeavour.

Speed of light

Light moves at 299,792,458m/s.

Star

A star is a large ball of searing hot gas, of which the **Sun** is one example. Many stars are millions of kilometres across, although they may only appear as pinpoints of light to us. (*See also:* **Stellar**.)

Stars may be immensely old, but they are always changing. By looking at many stars, astronomers have been able to piece together the life story of a star.

This is what happens:

▶ **Star** – The life and death of a star.

1 – The space between stars contains gas and dust. It can gather into clouds known as nebulae. When enough gas and dust collect in a nebula, it quickly collapses into one or more stars. The gas and dust are drawn ever more closely into a tight ball by the effects of gravity. The fusion that takes place releases enormous amounts of heat. Eventually, it becomes hot enough to shine.

Star begins to grow

2, 3 – During much of its life a star burns hydrogen gas by fusion and shines brightly, and little change appears to happen.

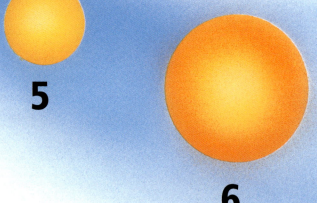

▲ **Space Shuttle** – The Space Shuttle was designed to be an all-purpose reusable space vehicle. It is currently helping to build the International Space Station.

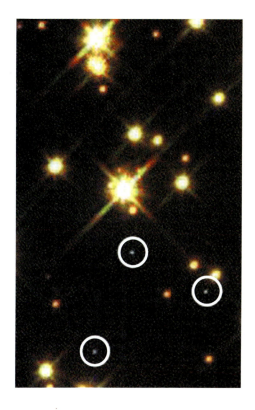

▶ **Star** – Three white dwarf stars (circled) among a star cluster, M4, of brighter yellow sun-like stars and cooler **red dwarf** stars.

Stellar

Anything relating to the **stars**. Interstellar refers to the part of space between the stars.

4, 5, 6, 7 – Eventually, the hydrogen fuel is used up, and only helium is left to burn. Since helium burns at much higher temperatures than hydrogen, the star gets brighter. At the same time, the outer part of the star begins to expand again, forming a red giant star. Eventually, the star literally blows apart and produces the spectacular 'fireworks' in space called a supernova.

A supernova is a red giant that explodes. It suddenly increases in brightness by a factor of many billions, but even within a few weeks it begins to fade. The Crab Nebula (some 7,000 light-years away) consists of material ejected by the supernova of 1054.

A supernova may radiate more energy in a few days than the Sun does in 100 million years. The stellar remnant left behind after the explosion is a star only a few kilometres in diameter but with an enormously high density.

8, 9, 10, 11 – The remnant star then contracts as a neutron star or white dwarf, spinning quickly and sending out pulses of radio waves like a galactic beacon. That is why a neutron star is also sometimes called a pulsar. Eventually the neutron star dies, its heat is lost and it ceases to shine. Although it still exists in the galaxy, it can no longer be seen and it is now called a black dwarf.

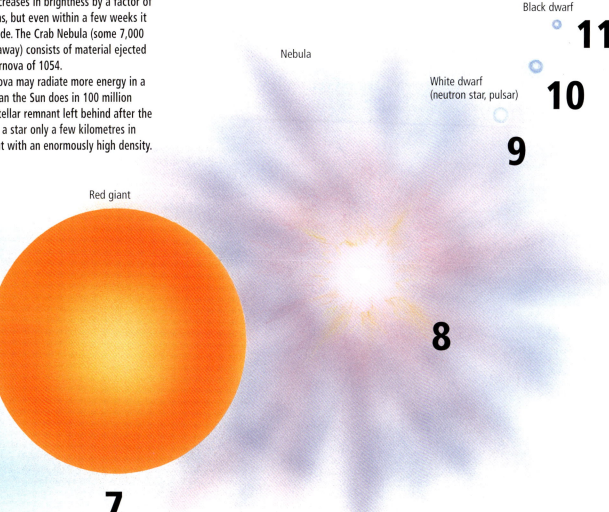

Nebula

Black dwarf

11

White dwarf
(neutron star, pulsar)

10

9

Red giant

8

7

Sun, the

The Sun is a **star** 1.4 million km across with gases that constantly churn over and send huge streams of matter far out into the **Universe**.

We receive just one two-millionths of all the energy emitted by the Sun, and yet plants can still capture enough of it to provide the energy for all life on **Earth**, nearly 150 million km away.

The Sun is so large that it has immense gravitational pull and can hold all nine **planets** of the **Solar System** in orbit.

(*For more on the Sun see:*
Chromosphere; **Corona**;
Diamond ring; **Eclipse**; **Filament**;
Flare; **Photosphere**; **Prominence**;
Solar wind; **Sunspot**.)

▶ **The Sun** – The Sun, showing the main parts of its structure.

Sunspots (dark) and faculae (light). They show where the Sun is turning over its gases most actively. In any one region they last for between a few weeks and several months. Sunspot activity is linked to the Sun's magnetism and varies in a cycle lasting 22 years.

The Sun spins once on its axis every 25 days.

Corona. This is the region of thin, intensely hot gases that spread beyond the visible Sun, and that is picked out as the faint glow that extends beyond the Sun and can be seen during an eclipse. It is the Sun's version of an atmosphere.

Prominences and flares. These gigantic solar fireworks are produced when the incredibly powerful magnetic fields of the Sun pull glowing gases away from its surface. They are most common when the sunspot activity is greatest.

▼ **The Sun** – This picture shows the churning motions of the cauldron that is the Sun.

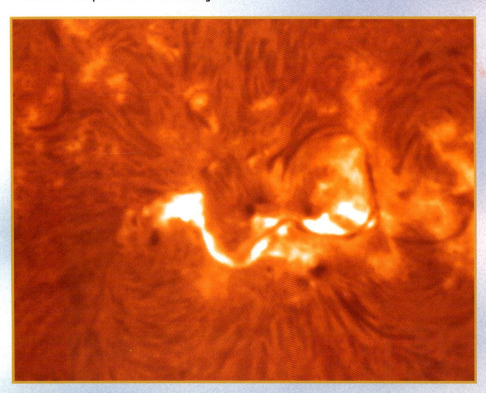

The yellow colour of the Sun is caused by its temperature. It glows yellow (almost white hot) because its surface is at about 6,000°C.

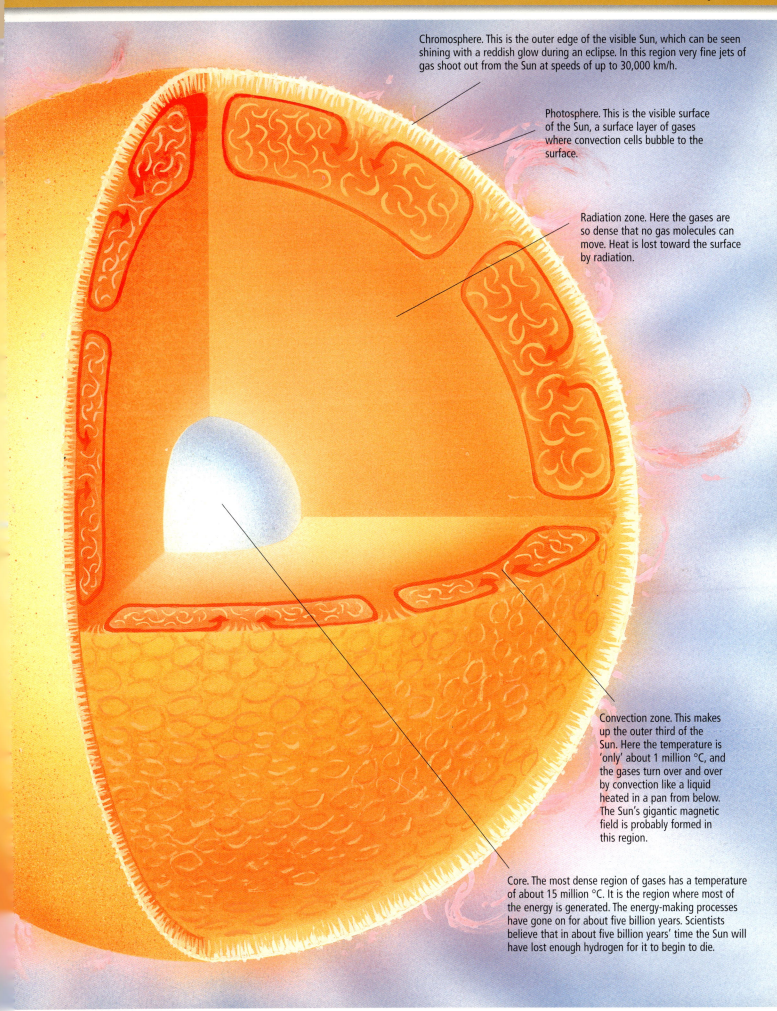

Chromosphere. This is the outer edge of the visible Sun, which can be seen shining with a reddish glow during an eclipse. In this region very fine jets of gas shoot out from the Sun at speeds of up to 30,000 km/h.

Photosphere. This is the visible surface of the Sun, a surface layer of gases where convection cells bubble to the surface.

Radiation zone. Here the gases are so dense that no gas molecules can move. Heat is lost toward the surface by radiation.

Convection zone. This makes up the outer third of the Sun. Here the temperature is 'only' about 1 million °C, and the gases turn over and over by convection like a liquid heated in a pan from below. The Sun's gigantic magnetic field is probably formed in this region.

Core. The most dense region of gases has a temperature of about 15 million °C. It is the region where most of the energy is generated. The energy-making processes have gone on for about five billion years. Scientists believe that in about five billion years' time the Sun will have lost enough hydrogen for it to begin to die.

Sunspot

An area seen as a dark spot on the **photosphere** of the **Sun**. It is a region of slightly cooler gas.

Superior planets

The **planets Mars**, **Jupiter**, **Saturn**, **Uranus**, **Neptune** and **Pluto** are called superior planets because their **orbits** are farther from the **Sun** than **Earth's** orbit.

Supernova

A violent explosion that occurs at the end of the life of some **stars**. When it explodes, the star may, for a brief time of a few weeks, be a billion times brighter than the **Sun**.

Surveyor

A series of **NASA** probes that landed on the **Moon** between 1966 and 1968 to gather information before the **Apollo project** began.

T

Titan

The largest moon of **Saturn** and the second largest moon in the **Solar System** (*see:* **Moons**). It is 5,150km across and is the only moon to have an **atmosphere**. Titan's atmosphere is made up mainly of nitrogen.

▼ **Supernova** – Red dust surrounding these star clusters was probably created by supernovae explosions. At the top left is a red supernova remnant, N57D.

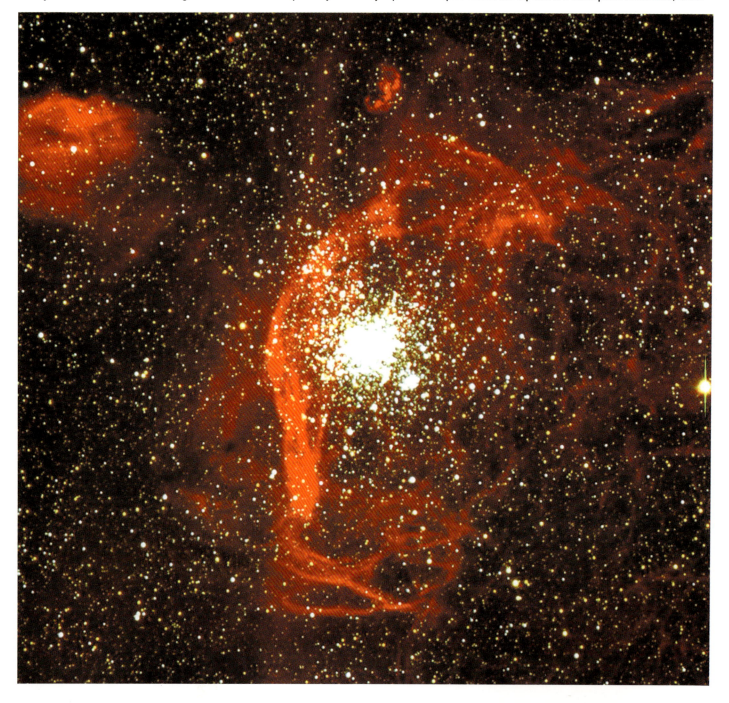

Triton

The largest moon of **Neptune**, some 2,706km across (*see:* **Moons**). It has an icy surface, but there are huge geyser-like eruptions, possibly of liquid nitrogen.

U

Umbra

The dark central region of an **eclipse**.

Universe

Everything that exists. The most popular theory of the origin of the Universe is the **Big Bang** theory. The known Universe is thought to have an age of about 20 billion years. (*See also:* **Cosmos** and **Expanding Universe**.)

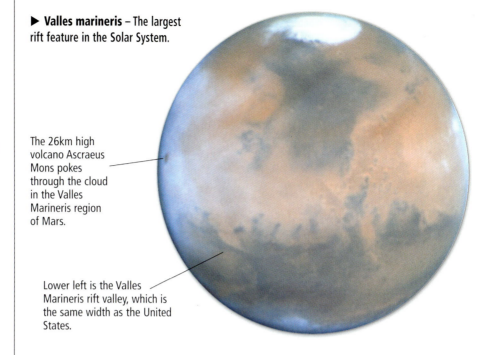

▶ **Valles marineris** – The largest rift feature in the Solar System.

The 26km high volcano Ascraeus Mons pokes through the cloud in the Valles Marineris region of Mars.

Lower left is the Valles Marineris rift valley, which is the same width as the United States.

Uranus

Uranus (diameter 51,100km) is the seventh **planet** of the **Solar System**. It is about four times the diameter and 15 times the **mass** of the **Earth**, and orbits the **Sun** every 84 years at a distance of 2.9 billion km. It spins on its **axis** in just over 17 hours.

Uranus has an impenetrable **atmosphere** of 83% hydrogen, 15% helium and 2% methane, which is over 8,000km thick. Beneath it is an ocean of hot water over 10,000km deep. The solid part of the planet is made of rock and is about the same size as the Earth. At the centre is a core of molten rock. A system of

11 faint rings surrounds the planet. Uranus has five major **moons** and ten smaller ones. (*See also:* **Ariel**; **Miranda**; **Voyager**.)

Uranus is unusual in that its axis is in its plane of **orbit**, that is, it 'spins on its back'. This may have been caused by an ancient collision with another planet. (*See also:* **Herschel, (Frederik) William**.)

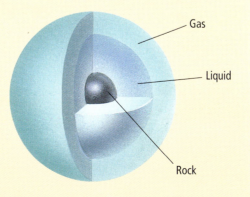

Gas

Liquid

Rock

V

Valles Marineris

A spectacular canyon on **Mars**, equal in length to the width of the United States and the largest rift feature in the **Solar System**.

Van Allen belts

Two radiation belts surrounding the **Earth**. They were discovered by James Van Allen in 1945. (*See also:* **Explorer**.)

Vega

The common name for the **star** Alpha Lyrae, the fifth brightest in the sky (*see:* **Brightest stars**).

◀ **Uranus** – The structure of Uranus is similar to Neptune, with helium–hydrogen atmosphere surrounding a liquid helium and hydrogen 'mantle' over a small rocky core.

Venus

Venus (diameter 12,100km) is the second **planet** from the **Sun**. It is 108 million km from the Sun, orbiting once every 225 days and spinning clockwise on its **axis** once every 243 days.

It is known as the evening and morning 'star' in our skies and is about the same size as the **Earth**. However, it is one of the most hostile environments in the **Solar System**. The shining white 'surface' of the planet is actually an **atmosphere** containing carbon dioxide and sulphur-dioxide rich clouds. From the clouds a rain of sulphuric acid droplets continually falls on the rocky surface.

The atmosphere absorbs heat from the Sun, so that the air temperature is about 480°C (a kind of extreme form of the Earth's 'greenhouse effect'), and it is actually hotter than **Mercury**, a planet much closer to the Sun.

The atmosphere also protects the surface from all but a few **meteoroids**, so the surface does not have as many **craters** as, for example, **Mars**.

It is believed that Venus contains a molten core similar to that of the Earth. The rocks on Venus are also similar to those found on the Earth's continents (granite) and below the Earth's oceans (basalt). Venus does not have a magnetic field, but it probably once had oceans of water – before the 'greenhouse effect' caused them to boil away. (*See also:* **Magellan**; **Mariner**.)

▲ **Venus** – Magellan, the probe that photographed Venus.

Rocky crust

Mantle

Core

▼▲ **Venus** – The evening and morning star reflects light well and so appears white. It is, in fact, a yellow–brown planet with a crust, a mantle and a core not unlike those on the Earth. The core is probably solid because Venus does not show any signs of having a magnetic field.

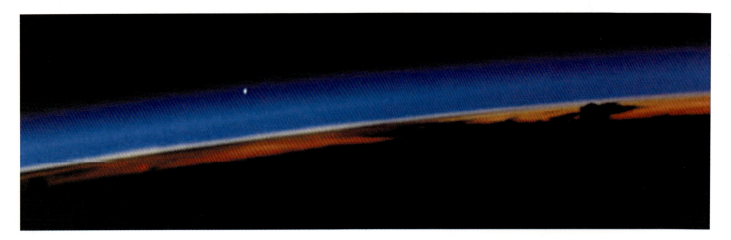

▲ **Viking** – The Viking lander.

Viking

A series of two **NASA** space probes to **Mars**.

Voyager

A series of two **NASA** probes to the outer **planets**. They were planned for launch in 1977 in order to make use of a special **conjunction** of the outer planets. The Voyager probe mission is ongoing.

▶ **Voyager** – This shows a full-scale model of the Voyager spacecraft. On the right is the science boom, containing cameras and other instruments. The long boom at left has two magnetic-field detectors and stretches 14m out from the spacecraft. In the centre is an antenna 4m in diameter, providing communication with Earth. Below is a shiny gold disc, a record called "Sounds of Earth," with messages and pictures from our planet.

W

Weight

The gravitational force exerted on a body.

White dwarf

A whitish **star** of high surface temperature and low brightness, with a **mass** approximately equal to that of the Sun but with a density many times larger.